THE LADY IS A GENERAL

Books by Cindy Jacobs

Deliver Us from Evil

The Supernatural Life

Possessing the Gates of the Enemy

The Power of Persistent Prayer

Women, Rise Up!

The Essential Guide to the Prophetic

The Lady Is a General

THE LADY IS A GENERAL

Lessons from a Trailblazing Prophet's Call to Shape Nations

CINDY JACOBS

Chosen
a division of Baker Publishing Group
Minneapolis, Minnesota

Published by Chosen Books
Minneapolis, Minnesota
ChosenBooks.com

Chosen Books is a division of
Baker Publishing Group, Grand Rapids, Michigan

Printed in the United States of America

Library of Congress Cataloging-in-Publication Data
Names: Jacobs, Cindy, 1951– author
Title: The lady is a general : lessons from a trailblazing prophet's call to shape nations / Cindy Jacobs.
Description: Minneapolis, Minnesota : Chosen Books, a division of Baker Publishing Group, [2026] | Includes biographical information. | Includes bibliographical references. | Audience term: Christians
Identifiers: LCCN 2026011429 | ISBN 9780800773496 cloth | ISBN 9781493483228 ebook
Subjects: LCSH: Jacobs, Cindy, 1951– | Christian biography—United States | LCGFT: Autobiographies
Classification: LCC BR1725.J3195 A3 2026
LC record available at https://lccn.loc.gov/2026011429

Stories told in this book reflect the author's present recollections of experiences over time. Some names and characteristics have been changed, some events have been compressed, and some dialogue has been recreated.

Cover design by Peter Gloege, Look Design Studio
Photography by Rocky Jordan

Baker Publishing Group publications use paper produced from sustainable forestry practices and postconsumer waste whenever possible.

26 27 28 29 30 31 32 7 6 5 4 3 2 1

This book is dedicated to my husband,
Michael Gaines Jacobs.

I would never have become the person I am today,
nor would I have accomplished all I have done,
without your love and support.
We have been through life's challenges
and the ups and downs of pioneering together.
You're my hero and will forever be the love of my life.

Contents

Introduction

Reasons for Writing My Memoirs

How does a person write the story of one's life? That is a big task. I must admit, most people probably struggle when thinking of taking on such a daunting challenge. As I have written, I keep remembering one more story and then another. What you have before you, however, is lovingly written for you, the reader!

I remember discussing this very subject of memoirs with my mentor, Peter Wagner. Those around him were encouraging him to write his memoirs, including me. I'll never forget the sincerity in his voice when he said to me, "Cindy, I wrote a book on humility, and it doesn't seem to be humble to write a book about yourself."

Now I understand! The act of writing about oneself feels strange, not only the humility part, but also the act of introspection it requires. What does one leave in? What is too private for me to share? What do I share with integrity, without hurting people who were in the middle of the situations and their families?

I did learn some things through the years that would be helpful to share with others who are pioneering in ministry. Being a forerunner as a woman in ministry and pioneering in that area often left me with a lot of questions, without having the luxury of being able to ask those who had walked that way before me. Many friends whom I came to know were pastoring with their husbands. Thank the Lord that God gave me Mike, my husband, to make the journey with me.

It is sad to say that, as far as women being allowed to stand in the pulpit, according to the latest statistics I could find as I write this, at least 33 percent of churches in America still will not allow a woman to preach. The numbers expand if you look at charismatics and even some Pentecostal denominations, who do not believe that a woman can have a place of authority over a man. (Note that some of their leaders might even have a female boss at a workplace.) For those of you who have questions about women in ministry, I wrote a whole book on the subject called *Women, Rise Up!*

Mike and I learned to work together, at times having very "spirited" discussions. Even women who are in business with their husbands know this can be a challenge. Most women in ministry whom I met after I was in ministry for a while did not work side by side with their husbands, so they couldn't give me any advice. Others were single and did not have the issues of learning about how the vision of the ministry would be set with someone you're married to! It is quite exciting for me to see how many leaders from the next generation are sharing in ministry now, side by side.

I believe that all women are called to be in ministry. It will just look different for each one of us. If you are a man reading this book, there is more to it than a story about one woman in ministry. You will find many mentoring principles to learn in its pages. If you are someone who has been longing for a mentor, this book should help you, whether you are getting started along life's path or are more seasoned.

It is my heartfelt prayer that you will visit with me as I am writing. I hope you feel like you are journeying with me, possibly even years after I've gone to heaven! I desire to help you finish your calling in life well. I want that for you.

Many rich blessings!

1

Early Days

I was born in the Baptist hospital in downtown San Antonio, Texas, on August 25, 1951. Mom and Dad told me my birth was an answer to their prayers. My parents had lost a baby before me, and they earnestly prayed for a little sister for my big brother, Richard. Perhaps that is why the Lord has used me to mobilize prayer around the world. Prayer begets prayer!

I was shy as a child. People have a hard time believing that now. We have a picture of me sitting on a couch, sucking my thumb. Yes, both shy and a thumb sucker! I would actually hide behind Mama when anyone came into the house.

People have asked me if I exhibited any supernatural abilities at a young age that foretold my prophetic gift. The answer is yes. But we did not know about prophecy at all. So I don't know what my mother thought when I was four years old and declared, "Mama, I'm going to have a baby sister." She did not yet know she was pregnant, and just patted me on the head and said, "No, honey, we are not having any more children. You are the last one." My sister, Lucy, was my parents' graduation present from seminary.

From the Gangs to the Gospel

A little background on my parents, Albert and Eleanor Johnson, and my grandparents, Albert and Emma Johnson on the paternal side, and George and Lucile McJilton on the maternal side. Each of them left a legacy and enriched my life story, as you will see.

My dad's family was all very tall. That could have been related to a Viking bloodline. Daddy was the shortest of his three brothers at five feet eleven inches. He also had a sister who was a model in New York who died early of cancer. I am not sure how Grandfather Johnson died. I just know that he was very tall, perhaps six feet eleven inches. I was told he used to wrestle alligators in the Everglades of Florida and was a blacksmith.

Dad lost his father when he was eleven. After my grandfather passed away, the family moved to Hell's Kitchen in New York City. Hell's Kitchen was the roughest of the rough part of New York, and it affected my dad. He had a Southern accent from being born in Savannah, Georgia, and he was fair game for the gangs to beat him up. He finally joined one for self-defense because he was tired of getting beaten up and having his toys taken away. It was survival.

Preaching the gospel was not on Dad's radar. I think he was mostly involved in petty thievery. The gang he joined was not as violent as some we have today.

Dad went to Aviation High School in New York and learned to work on airplanes. He and his big brother, Cecil, were also excellent dancers on a professional level, and they would dance together in clubs doing a doubles act.

There is no telling where my father would have ended up as a fatherless kid, but God intervened. One day as a young man, Dad heard the gospel preached on the streets of New York by Salvation Army evangelists, and he got gloriously saved and changed. From there, he gave up the gang life and started playing the trombone in the Salvation Army Band on 33rd Street and Broadway. He was mentored by a Presbyterian pastor and started preaching in that denomination.

Dad joined the United States Army Air Corps and was sent to San Antonio, Texas, for training. He met my mom at a USO recreation club for soldiers. She felt it was her "patriotic duty" to go dance with the soldiers who were going to fight in the war. Mom was a flaming redhead and had quite a charismatic personality. Despite having been born with a club foot, she loved to dance.

Mom was the opposite of Dad in many ways. She was a raised-in-church girl, and he came out of the gang life. She was a Presbyterian, too, so that worked. He was dating her girlfriend when they met, but that soon ceased.

Sunny and the Southern Belle

My maternal grandparents, George and Lucile McJilton, had moved to Oak Cliff, Texas, near Dallas, for George's work as an electrical engineer. It is said that his engineering books were in German because his family had immigrated from Germany to Philipsburg, Montana. Granddad helped install the first phone systems in America on the military bases during World War II. He died a few months before I was born, so I never knew him.

My grandmother, Lucile, was a pioneer schoolteacher from Iowa. She taught in a one-room classroom. When she was in college, a rarity for women in that era, she sold the *Book of*

Knowledge door-to-door to earn money. Her horse had formerly been used by the fire brigade, and whenever the bell rang for a fire, he would take off running toward the sound.

I do know that Grandfather McJilton was a burly football player nicknamed Sunny. He was brilliant and handsome. Grandmother was lovely and quite the catch. She and her sister, Louise, were raised by an aunt because both of their parents had died. They called Grandmother and her sister "the belles of Ottumwa, Iowa." I remember her telling me that they wore white rice powder for makeup. She met my grandfather at the state university. The story goes that she got cold feet the day before they married, but my granddad told her that was ridiculous and she should just marry him—and she did.

After their marriage, my maternal grandparents moved around the country while Granddad installed the first phone systems for military bases for the civil service. Their move to San Antonio was how my mother ended up in Texas. One night in Oak Cliff, near Dallas, my mama, around twenty years old at the time, was walking home from the trolley stop when two men stopped her, pulled a gun, and pointed it straight at her. She looked at them and announced, "I don't have time for this!" She turned her back on them and flounced away. I am so glad that God protected her, because that would have been the end of her life, and I would not exist! (Moral of the story: Don't mess with a redheaded woman!)

"Why Don't We Get Married?"

Dad was exuberant and quite a cutup. In those days, the army didn't allow GIs to stop and sit on park benches, to keep them out of trouble. Of course, my parents did sit for a kiss, and the military police showed up. When the MPs beamed their spotlight on them, Daddy jumped up on the picnic table and did a dance called a soft shoe. I don't think the MPs were impressed.

Mom also said that one day she was getting ready for a date at the boardinghouse where she lived. By the time she got downstairs, Daddy had all the girls in the house lined up, doing calisthenics!

Mama wrote Daddy when he was stationed in Okinawa during the war. He was a chaplain's assistant, an airplane mechanic, and a medic. Dad loved airplanes! It is interesting that my husband, Mike, is quite an airplane fanatic too.

When Dad got home from the war, Mom said, "Albert, why don't we get married?" Maybe she was prompted by Daddy lining up the girls to do exercises in her boardinghouse. At any rate, he agreed, and they married at the First Presbyterian Church in Oak Cliff. It is interesting that after many years of marriage, Mike and I moved to the Dallas area, about twenty minutes from where they got married.

When Mama was pregnant with my brother, they moved to San Antonio, and Daddy got connected to the Southern Baptists. Grandfather McJilton had died, and they went to live with my maternal grandmother and help her. Grandmother Lucile was quite a Southern lady who never wore a pair of slacks all her life. And she never left the house without her white gloves on and a pretty hat, not even going to the grocery store. She helped raise me for several years and also helped us financially.

One day, to my mother's horror, Daddy said they were leaving the Presbyterian church and becoming Southern Baptists. She could hardly believe it! To make matters worse, she had been sprinkled as a child and would have to be rebaptized. She finally conceded, from both love for the Lord and love for my daddy.

She was pregnant with my older brother, so my family has always said that both she and my brother got baptized twice.

Dad went to college on the GI Bill, through which the government provided an education to all the service people as a reward for serving. He chose to go to Baylor University in Waco, Texas. In those days you had to graduate from college and then go to seminary to be a Baptist preacher. So off we went to Baylor University. Again my grandmother helped us with food and housing. God sent her to help us!

After Baylor, Daddy went to Southwestern Theological Seminary in Fort Worth. The little house we lived in leaned and has subsequently been torn down. But something very special happened there. It was there that I gave my first prophecy, when I was four years old. As I mentioned earlier, Mom was pregnant with my baby sister, Lucy, and didn't know it.

After graduation from seminary, Daddy wanted to start churches right away and work with the Home Mission Board as a church planter. They thought their plate was full with two children, but God knew they needed a third!

2

A Family of Spiritual Pioneers

Pioneering requires a certain kind of courage and bravery. Church planters have a specific, unique calling. Who would want to move their family across many states, from Texas, the Bible Belt of America, to the East Bay of San Francisco in 1956? At the time, that part of America had very few churches and was vastly underserved. I now realize Dad was an apostle, but we didn't use those titles from Ephesians back then. You were either a pastor, a missionary, or an evangelist.

God had supernaturally opened a door to us. But the call to become a family of spiritual pioneers came with very little provision. Thank God for Grandmother McJilton, as close as one could get to an earthly angel. As I stated earlier, my maternal grandfather was an electrical engineer. He died at fifty-six years of age, but he had been strategic in his investments. In other words, his wife, Lucile, had some money. While she was very frugal on a personal level, she was extremely generous in helping my mother and father and our growing family.

After my mother passed away, I found a letter from Mama to her mama when my parents were planting a work in Shore Acres, California. The contents hit me deeply as I quietly read its words. Mama wrote, "Thank you so much for the coats that you sent us. It is cold and damp here, and we have suffered from it without proper clothing. Thank you also for the vitamins, as the children have all had the sniffles."

We were so loved by Grandmother Lucile. She was the only grandparent we had after her husband, George, passed away. As I mentioned earlier, my father's six-foot-eleven-inch dad, Albert, had died when Dad was eleven, and then his mother, Emma, also died early (in her fifties) of cancer. Grandfather McJilton, on my mother's side, died the Easter before I was born. Even though we had only one grandparent left, she made up for any lack.

I went to see my grandmother just before she passed away, at almost ninety-nine years of age. I heard her talking when I entered the room, as she lay on her bed at the nursing home. With her eyes closed, not knowing that I was listening, she said with a strong voice, "What is right and what is wrong? To love God with your whole heart, soul, and mind—that is what is right!"

God, the master weaver, has woven those last words into my being. Other words, like the prayers Daddy would pray when we knelt down by the bed at night, were woven in too. He had a big, booming voice. He had huge hands and wore a size 13 ring and size 13 shoes. Daddy was a man of prayer. He prayed over us, over his congregation, and for souls, souls, souls.

All in a Day's Work

The work in Shore Acres was a challenge from the beginning. First of all, the city council voted that they did not want a church in their city. To my fiery parents, this was, as we say here in Texas, like saying "Sic 'em" to a dog. That only made them want to plant the work more.

One day, my parents were driving down the street, and Mom pointed out an old farmhouse to Daddy. It was for rent. They parked, got out, and started walking over the land. It was a big mess! It stank of cow and horse manure. The barn and old farmhouse were run-down and badly in need of repair. The best thing about it was that it was on the other side of the street from the city limits. They went for it and got a lease.

Shoveling manure, picking up trash, tearing down walls to reconfigure the farmhouse, and such are all in a day's work for pioneers. After we started the church, Dad preached like he was ministering to thousands. He would preach some wild illustrated sermons. One time, he had a coffin brought in and jumped out of it in a sermon on the resurrection.

Facing Crises as a Family

The spiritual poverty of the areas we pioneered in was deep and wide. I had a friend whose father hanged himself one night. Daddy got the call and went to stay with the family until the police arrived. He stayed afterward too. What does one tell a family after such a tragedy? Daddy came home late that night, very quiet and white.

Satan fought us tooth and nail as we pushed back and took away his territory. One day when I was in first grade, I walked up the street to the elementary school. It was a straight shot up the road. Suddenly, a big black dog chased a cat right between my legs! The result was that I was flipped up into the air, and I landed in the middle of the street. To my horror, a car was speeding toward me and barely stopped in time before it ran me over! I remember looking up at the tires right next to my body.

Another time, I ran out of our house and straight into the sharp corner of a window that rolled open by a knob from the inside. The window cut my head rather deeply. We had a problem then, as Dad had gone somewhere. Although he had left the car, Mom was just learning to drive and had no driver's license. But being the fiery redhead that she was, Mama did not let that deter her from saving her baby! We made it to the doctor in time for me to be saved with minimal blood loss and a few stitches.

Another potentially critical situation came when my kindergarten class was learning choreography. I danced myself right off the high stage and somehow survived!

The last potentially life-threatening situation that I remember was when a brush fire started in the vacant lot behind our house. It roared out of control quickly, as it was dry grass and weeds. We watered our yard to the best of our ability, but the fire stopped just short of burning down our home. There is never a dull moment when one pioneers!

Riveted by Daddy's Shoes

It is hard for me to ascertain how much to share with you of my family's story or my growing-up days. I have prayed that God would guide me, however, so I am trusting that these nuances of my life will touch you in some way. One particularly poignant snapshot of my daddy's prayer life I want to share came when we lived in Yuma, Arizona. That was a particularly trying time for us. We lived in a tar paper–covered parsonage in an extremely hot climate. Dad had installed temporary evaporative air-conditioning. (For those of you not familiar with that kind of cooling unit, it was a fan that blew over water. Pretty effective in that kind of weather.) For some reason, one day my six-year-old self decided to go across the way, to the church. I probably wanted to ask my daddy for a favor. As I entered the sanctuary through the swinging double doors, I felt a holy hush. My daddy, without knowing I was there, was kneeling at the altar, praying out loud.

I do not recall his prayer, but what was stamped into my young mind was the picture of his shoes. They had big holes in them. Somehow, I had not seen the bottom of my handsome father's shoes before—only the tops, which were always shiny (probably due to his military background).

Dad's shoes riveted me. How could my daddy have holes in his shoes? Questions spilled across my mind. Were we too poor to buy him new ones or get his old ones fixed?

Shoes were rather a big deal in our family, as money was tight. My feet are narrow, and we used to drive one hundred miles to Austin to buy my shoes. And they were expensive! The ones that fit me looked orthopedic. (I remember my fourth-grade schoolteacher asking me if I was a special needs student because of the kind of shoes I wore.) I had one pair of shoes for school and one pair for Sundays, and I dared not scuff them, knowing how dear they were to buy. Yet Dad always made sure I had shoes that fit my feet properly, even when his own had holes in the bottom.

Years later, a friend took me to buy a pair of shoes for my birthday. When I got home, I was stunned to find out how expensive they were. The still, small voice of the Lord whispered into my heart, *Cindy, I saw your daddy's shoes too. Your daddy couldn't buy you nice shoes, but I can see you receive them!* To this day, people buy me the nicest shoes without my ever asking!

A Childhood on the Move

As I said earlier, pioneering was hard. We moved to the small town of Flatonia, Texas, where most of the people were Czech-Catholics, and the Baptist pastor's daughter got picked on. When I think of it, I don't think my teacher there liked Baptists very much either. She asked me what was wrong with my hair because it was so bushy. My hair is curly, and Mama cut it at home to save money, and it did tend to stick out.

Even though we did not have many things, Mom and Dad could always throw a party. I think it was more Mama than Daddy, but he always heartily entered in. One Christmas, we did not have many presents under the tree, but Mama and Daddy had bought balloons of animal characters, like Mickey Mouse, and each balloon had cardboard feet. We had a ball playing with those balloons. I think the little things my parents did were why I never felt poor, even though we were.

My brother, Richard, and I recently talked about the number of times we moved during our childhood. Part of the reason was that, between church plants, Daddy did fill-in work. We would drive to small towns outside of a big city where we lived, such as San Antonio, and he would preach on Sunday morning and Sunday night, and then we drove home again.

The Baptists were never just a "go to church once on Sunday" people. Sunday was a big deal. Of course, we were very strict about leaving church on time—right at noon. There were pot roasts in the oven, biscuits to make, and a quick nap to take before we went back for the evening service and Training Union (a youth discipleship ministry). After those night services, we would bundle ourselves into the car and drive home again.

Friends Are Like Family

I distinctly remember how I began to feel lonely, moving around so much. I already mentioned that I was shy. There came a monumental moment in my young life when I decided I was going to make friends quickly everywhere we moved, and I did. To this day, I so value my friendships, and once someone becomes my friend, that person also becomes like family. People have to do something awful or break the friendship from their end for it to be over. I am so blessed to have dear, dear friends today.

Friends are covenantal to me. Many are my family. One doesn't just throw away a family member because they hurt your feelings. A true friendship has both give and take. Of course, I found out that some people are mostly takers. One day, my little sister, Lucy, called me after she moved with her husband, Mark Riethmiller, to Minnesota from Texas. "I'm so lonely," she said. "Nobody wants to be my friend!"

I was the big sister, and I always kind of mothered my baby sister. I needed to help her. "Let's pray!" I boomed in my best big sister voice. We earnestly agreed for friends for her.

Lucy was a degreed, trained counselor. At first, it seemed like many friends came, but they ate up her time, just wanting advice. I told her, "Let them go! They are takers. Friendship is always tit-for-tat. You give, and they do too." Our prayers shifted to, "Father, bring her true friends who want to give as well as take." And it happened! After that, she got the best friends who were with her through the trials of life and stayed with her every step.

Friends cry with you when you cry, let you vent until you get it all out, and don't think any less of you. They are also good listeners. When you call them, weeping over a betrayal or a tragedy, they know the right things to say or not say. They literally mourn with those who mourn, and weep with those who weep (see Romans 12:15). In addition, friends can be strong when you need to shape up your attitude, without fear that you will walk away. These friends might be from school, a job, or church. The best friendships are those that stay with you season after season, year after year, with the passing of time.

Mentors to Model After

Between church plants, our family would move back to San Antonio, where Grandma Lucile lived. We would joke that this was where we went to "lick our wounds" from our last adventures in pioneering. I cannot tell you what a safe place it was for us, and especially for me. Grandma was the one who took care of me when we moved in with her after Grandfather McJilton died. He passed in April, before I was born on August 22, 1951. Mama and Daddy both had to work, and Richard was in school.

As you can tell, Grandma was a central figure in my life, who molded me greatly. In many ways, I modeled myself after her. She was a lady; I wanted to be a lady. Her house was always neat and tidy, and beautiful. When I was a young person, I would often clean my room, and my brother's and sister's rooms too. Like my grandmother, I valued order. She loved to grow roses and garden, and a beautiful garden makes my heart soar. Of course, both my parents had good work ethics as well. I cannot overstate the way they influenced me.

When I am mentoring someone today, I always look for the one who goes beyond what he or she is asked to do. We have often hired such volunteers as full-time staff after seeing their work ethic. I have found that proactive people make amazing ministers and workers. When I am praying for people, they are the ones who watch what I am doing. They show up where I am ministering without being asked. Who you are is often revealed by your actions.

As they say, talk is cheap. One needs to be a disciple and servant first. Years ago, I would drive Vinita Copeland (Kenneth Copeland's mother) around when she would preach. And when she held Monday night meetings at a hotel in Fort Worth, Mike and I would walk her to her car and make sure she was all right and safe. Nobody asked us to do that. It was simply part of honoring her, both as a minister and a mentor, and being a servant to a great woman of God. As the apostle Paul said, "I will show you my faith by my works" (James 2:18).

3

A Clean Heart and the Call to Ministry

When I was five years old, we visited a church when Daddy was between pastorates. The Sunday school teacher gave a lesson about salvation. She showed us two hearts. One was a beautiful, clean white heart. The other was very ugly and dark. The first one depicted a life when Jesus forgave our sin and we were His children, and the second one depicted a life without Christ. I cannot tell you what happened, other than I had a supernatural visitation from God. I knew I was a sinner. I knew I needed that white heart. When my teacher asked who wanted to pray to have that white heart, my hand shot up! This is why I never say that a child cannot understand they need Jesus.

Later on, in "big church," as we called it, I begged Mom and Dad to let me go down to the front and tell people I was a Christian. I will never forget the song we were singing that bright Sunday morning: "Just as I am, without one plea, but that thy blood was shed for me."*

* "Just As I Am," lyrics by Charlotte Elliott, 1835, music by William Bradbury, 1849, public domain.

I wanted to get baptized right away, but my parents felt I needed to understand more about what was happening to me and said, "Not now, dear." I kept pestering my dad, until one day when I was the advanced age of seven, he agreed to baptize me. Our church did not have a baptistry, so we borrowed one. When it came time for me to be baptized, Daddy took my hand and floated me out to a big cement block that he had placed in the water for me to stand on. I wore my white baptismal gown, and the day felt altogether heavenly.

Music Moved Me Out of Shyness

I also begged for piano lessons when I was five years old. Every time I looked at a piano, I knew I wanted my fingers to make music. Of course, the cost was simply out of the question for our struggling family. My mom wrote to Grandmother McJilton, and she came through again for me! My first piano teacher told my mother that I couldn't play the piano because my hands were too small and I couldn't reach the pedals. Mom found another teacher. When we moved to Flatonia, I was in the third grade and discovered I was pretty good at playing the classics. That began my love for classical music and my journey toward what I thought would be a lifelong career in music.

My very first piano was lent to us by a fireman. It had been in the local firehouse and had a warped keyboard. That did not matter to me. It was a piano, and it was in my house! No more having to slip away to the church to practice.

One part of taking piano lessons is recitals. Even though I was shy, I could somehow manage to play for an auditorium full of people and even enjoyed it! Looking back, I always felt that I somehow belonged on that stage. It was as if I was seeing myself talking to crowds of people. This was actually more important for me, perhaps, than for others, because playing in recitals helped me with my shyness. Remember the picture I talked about earlier that showed I had a very noticeable bad habit as a young child? It was a sweet picture from my third birthday party that showed me with big brown eyes, but it also showed that I was a thumb sucker. (There, I said it again!) This all stemmed from shyness. When people came to our house, I would hide behind my mother's skirts, no doubt sucking that same thumb. Music brought me out from behind her skirts somehow.

Slowly, I overcame my shyness, partly thanks to those piano recitals. I would also teach Sunday school during my junior high days, mainly in the beginner's class, which also helped. We used big, colorful nineteen-by-twelve-inch pictures, and the lesson was printed on the back. Anyone could do that assignment, right? Wrong! Keeping those wiggling three- to five-year-old kids quiet when we had thin walls and the adult class was going on next door was not an easy task!

One thing that happens to people who write their memoirs is that it requires them to take time to reflect. How could I know that God was getting me ready to teach hundreds of thousands of people around the world by starting me out teaching children and ministering to a small missions church? It was all part of my training for my calling to the nations.

Living by Faith and Forgiveness

While pioneering spiritually, our family had some really tough financial times that marked my life. One evening, I recall us praying to have food to eat. That night our washing machine broke down, and when Daddy pulled it out and looked under it, there was a soggy ten-dollar bill. I guess he dried it out, because we bought groceries. Back then, Cokes were a nickel, candy bars were three cents, and one could get a really great soft-serve Dairy Queen ice cream for a nickel, and a double serve for ten cents. To this day, since ice cream was such a big treat, it is still our family's favorite comfort food. One day my husband, Mike, asked my sister and me what our favorite food was, and in a chorus Lucy and I emoted, "Ice cream!" (Not very good for the waistline, but I was pretty tiny years ago.)

We did learn how to live by faith. I had a good friend, Sally Horton, who was the dean of women at Christ For The Nations Institute in Dallas. She used to say with a chuckle, "I have been both abased [poor] and abounded [blessed]. I much prefer abounding!" Me too!

In 1962, Daddy moved the family to Phoenix, Arizona, to work with the Home Mission Board in church planting. I will never forget hearing that our salary was twenty-five dollars a week, hardly enough even then to feed a family of five. Through the years of starting over in various ways, we all pitched in to help. One year, it was by pulling our little red wagon piled high with telephone books to distribute. (Back then, everyone's number was published in a book. I recall we had a three-party line, meaning we shared it with three families, and we only had to dial four digits. There were no area codes. Not much information was private.) We made one dollar a book to pass them out. Doing the math, twenty-five books meant a week's salary!

Dad worked with a church that was established, but he began to get the itch to pioneer more. So we moved to an area called Maryvale. At that time, it was a brand-new housing division without a church. Dad found an old army barracks for sale and had it moved to a lot and outfitted for a church. By that time, I was getting good at playing the piano (again, thank you, Grandma), and I would play for our services.

After a while, another person accompanied our worship service, and I went to play for the Spanish-speaking church in nearby Tolleson. I think I was around thirteen and did that for about a year and a half. It was then that I fell in love with the Latino people and learned to make Mexican food—a fact that my husband is thankful for to this day!

There were days when I was sure my daddy felt like quitting. Satan prowled and growled and sometimes bit! Dad had been given a big pulpit Bible by his mother before she died. He proudly placed it with the pages open on the Lord's Supper table that stood in front of the pulpit. That Bible was beautiful, with big pictures of stories from God's Word. One day when Dad went to church by himself (probably to find a quiet place to pray), to his shock and sorrow, vandals had broken into the building. They had torn pages out of the Bible, scattered them around, and sprayed satanic graffiti on the Lord's Supper table! As far as I know, that was the only possession that his mother, my Grandma Johnson, had given him. It was such a loss! But Dad just cleaned up, painted over the words of disrespect, and kept preaching.

What did I learn from that? Perseverance! Tragedy can either make us strong or break us. Mom and Dad got stronger from that experience. They forgave, and we stood in their shadow and learned how to stand and not be shaken.

Our subdivision was called Starlight Park. It had cement block homes, and Dad could buy one, probably with a Veterans Administration loan that was part of the package given to our soldiers. We got a good deal on a house. Part of the reason, I think, was that it was a charcoal color, the only one on the block that color, and people knew it would be baking hot in the Phoenix sun. We didn't care, though. My parents made it a home. One good thing was that this new house was not next to the building, and people did not feel they had the right to walk through and inspect it. I found out later that my parents gave the house to the church as a parsonage. Church planting gives one the blessing of walking in forgiveness toward the congregation on a regular basis!

My parents both taught me to stay in a state of forgiveness. I will never forget the night I attended the required church business meeting. I must have been around sixteen. As usual, I sat in the back, writing notes to my friends. No texting then; we used hard copy! Suddenly, my attention was drawn to the business at hand. They were arguing over how much to pay my daddy. As I listened to the miserly attitudes of some of the people, I started to fume inside. The discussion centered around giving us a monthly raise of five dollars. I understood we struggled with our low pay as it was. I also knew Daddy had built most of the building we sat in with his bare hands.

Afterward, I found Mom talking to a lady who was the bane of the church, Mrs. Leatherberry (not her real name). Mrs. Leatherberry was complaining about my dad to my mom. She whined in a nasal voice, "Well, if your husband visited people more, we would have more members."

I stood behind Mama because she had taken my hand and pulled me behind her. I know you simply cannot believe it, but I had a strong-willed disposition. I stood with clenched fists, thinking, *Mama, if you just move a little more to the left, I am going to fix her face!*

To my chagrin, Mama looked at Mrs. Leatherberry very sweetly, and she calmly said, "Oh, I am so sorry you feel that way, because we love you so much!"

The wind went out of my sails right then. I learned another important lesson: "A soft answer turns away wrath" (Proverbs 15:1). I also learned humility. Did I have a right to take up an offense for my daddy? Absolutely! Would that have helped the situation? No. The Bible speaks about heaping coals of fire on your neighbor's head, meaning to give them a blessing of light to see their way home (see Romans 12:20). Mrs. Leatherberry's face displayed shame. She knew she had been mean-spirited, and my mother did not have to tell her that. God said it for Mama through her kindness. Once again, God forged His principles into my life through her actions.

The Calling to Ministry

I want to give this section to the special moment in my life when God called me to ministry. In fact, I've always felt that the place in which He touched my life was very important as well. Each summer, the children from our church would go to a very beautiful place in Prescott, Arizona, called Paradise Valley Ranch. I loved that place. The air was very fresh, as it was in the mountains, and one could smell the pine needles when you got near. The dorm rooms were as close to camping out as I personally prefer, and there was always the thrill of watching the daddy longlegs spiders bounce up and down the ceiling above your bunk. In fact, I used to play with them! One does not grow up in Texas without learning to play with, or at least tolerate, bugs.

What really marked my life there, other than the games and outdoor adventures, were lessons on pioneer missionaries. The summer of my ninth year, I simply devoured those stories. As we looked at pictures of people from other nations, my heart burst with a longing to be with them and know them. The afternoon after our mission's lesson, my teacher told us, "Go outside and find a place to talk to God."

I went behind the brown, wooden chapel and found a big rock. I realize, looking back now, that the presence of God surrounded me as a little girl. I prayed, *God, what do You want me to do with my life?* At that moment, the power of God touched my heart. The Lord made it clear that He had a calling for me and that I would understand more as I got older. It also seemed clear that God would give me a husband, and he would be involved in the calling as well.

In the chapel the next day, we all sang the specific song with a calling attached: "I have decided to follow Jesus; no turning back, no turning back."* The plaintive words were, to me, my confirmation that God wanted me to surrender my life to full-time service for God's Kingdom. My heart was beating fast as I made my way down the aisle with tears running down my face.

I "walked the aisle," as the Baptists say. After I got to the front, I was handed a card that gave me choices as to what I was surrendering my life to do. It listed Pastor, Evangelist, and Missionary. Well, in the Baptist church I could not be a pastor or evangelist, but I knew there were women missionaries, so that is what I signed up to do!

Now I know that was exactly the right box to check. God has given me a call to the nations, and while I am not a long-term missionary, Mike and I go to the nations pretty much on a monthly or even semimonthly basis each year, and we love it!

* The hymn "I Have Decided to Follow Jesus" reportedly originated with a Garo man named Nokseng, who became a Christian in India in the mid-nineteenth century and was martyred. He is said to have recited verses from John 12 as he and his family were killed. The formation of the martyr's words into a hymn has been attributed to the Indian missionary Sadhu Sundar Singh, but an alternative tradition attributes the hymn to Pastor Simon K. Marak.

Since that time, there are many things I have learned about following God's plan for one's life. I am honored you are taking this journey with me through my memories, so I can share with you some of the lessons I have learned.

4

Struggles and Joys

You have probably already imagined that I was a deep thinker and a rather melancholic child. It took me many years to discover that fact and work through the inherent weakness I had, and to develop a more balanced, Spirit-controlled temperament. I can tell you, at the onset, that this is not only possible to do, but part of God's plan for our lives.

One of the bondages in my life was, as I've mentioned, shyness. I cannot think of one situation that caused me to be so, but I did begin to understand it was definitely a weakness. It wasn't something I just overcame in one powerful moment. I learned to overcome it by following God's leading, moment by moment.

I did have a few traumas along the way related to being a pastor's kid. The subdivision where we lived in Maryvale, on the outskirts of Phoenix, was a tough one, even that long ago. There was a girl gang in my elementary school that took it upon themselves to make my life miserable. Being bullied is horrible. They discovered the route I took walking home and met me on the sidewalk one day. There must have been five of them. At first, they just taunted me. I put my head down and kept walking. They formed a circle around me and started to pull at my clothes. "How about we just take all these off of you right now?" they shouted, with voices that were filled with pure malice. For some reason, they thought it would be fun for the pastor's child to have to walk home without any clothes on. In the end, I started to run, and they gave up following me when I turned into a neighborhood.

At last, I got up the courage to tell my mom, who told my dad, and the jig was up for those gang girls! Dad stormed up to the school the next day and went straight to the principal's office. At that moment, as he was a former gang member himself who had grown up in Hell's Kitchen, the gloves came off! It was a good thing he was talking to the administration and not those mean girls. Somehow, Daddy got his point across. I was called in to recount my story, and I was never bothered by those girls again. Pastor Johnson could be so tender, but nobody, and I mean *nobody*, messed with his child!

Early Lessons in Learning to Lead

By the time I got to high school, I had been successful in certain areas of beating intimidation and the fear of man. I ran for office in what Maryvale High called Girl's Club. My freshman year, I was just a member. Every girl in the school was automatically a member of Girl's Club, and out of my school of four thousand, that was around half of the students.

My senior year, I ran for president. That meant I had to speak at a student-body assembly for the girls. What a big challenge, but certainly not the last one that I would face. One would have thought the bondage and intimidation were completely broken off me after that, but not so! More about that later.

To my delight, I won the election. Oh, the possibilities before me to make a difference in our school. There were also some really fun projects, like putting on the senior prom. Glancing back through the mirror of time, I can see that I learned organizational and people skills. I also must have been a bit overbearing, because the teacher who was the Girl's Club sponsor once said to me, "Cindy, you cannot expect to run the teachers at this school as well as the club!" Selah!

I have to be careful not to overstep myself in meetings today. Peter Wagner told me he had learned from John Maxwell to put a big *L* for *listen* on a piece of paper before meetings to help keep him from taking over. Of course, he was subtly telling me, "Cindy, you have a big mouth. Do not talk so much!" Peter also said, "How do you know that you have the gift of leadership? You turn around and everyone is following you." I must certainly have that, and it can run away with me if I am not aware.

While we are moving along this path, I loved the way Peter mentored me and others. He used what he called the sandwich method. First, he would say something complimentary, put the correction in the middle, and then finish up with another word of kindness.

My dad was much like Peter in that regard. One day when I was in second grade, I decided I was going to call him Father instead of Daddy or Dad. He stopped and looked at me and gently said, "Sweetheart, you have a Father who is in heaven. I am your daddy." Now I have my biological dad in heaven, and I still have Father God with me, and He watches out for me every day.

My being head of the organization putting on the prom presented a problem in my family. We were Baptist, and in those days,

Baptists did not dance! Nor did we play cards or go to the movie theater, at least not when I was little. The churches in the small towns like Flatonia were much stricter than in the bigger towns.

Daddy had once been a professional dancer onstage in New York City, and he was quite good. But that was when he was Presbyterian, so it was not a problem. He and his brother, Cecil, looked like twins and did duets on stage. When Dad told my mother he was going to change from being a Presbyterian to a Baptist, she cried! It meant a lot of changes, like not dancing.

Back to the prom situation. I had planned the prom, so I wanted to go to the prom. I had a date already, and my last hurdle was my dad. Mama said that I had to tell Daddy I wanted to go to the dance. Not only that, but it also meant Dad and Mom would have to come up with the money to buy me a long, formal dress, and money was scarce. I tried to pick the right time to have the dreaded conversation. One day, I found Dad lying down on the couch, looking tired, and I made the announcement: "Daddy, I want to go to the prom."

He gazed up with such profound sorrow and waited a moment. At last, he answered, "If that is what you want, then do it."

That was so hard, because I idolized my daddy. I now understand that I was starting, as a teenager, to individuate, or become my own person, and that included deciding what I believed. Daddy was so wise to let me find my own way, rather than shutting the door to my personal growth. I knew I was not sinning by going to that dance. But I would not have gone if he had said no, because I respected him so much.

Individuation, Questions, and More Questions

Speaking of individuation, that reminds me of the story of when our son, Daniel, had decided to grow his hair much longer than

I liked, and it blocked his vision somewhat. One day as I was driving him to school, he looked over and said, "Mom, I know you don't like my hair, but one day I will get tired of it and cut it." He did, in fact. While in Bible school, he shaved his whole head! (One's children can go from one extreme to the other in a few moments, so don't despair when they're only in a stage of life.)

I was always full of questions. I'd ask things like, "Why did God say we have to do things this way or that way?" Once when I was in just such a questioning mood, I got into one of the few loud fights I ever had with my mother. She ended up shouting, "Don't you believe the Bible?"

"Yes," I forcefully shouted back, "but I want to know the reason the Bible says that!"

Mama was crying by that time, at which point my daddy stormed in, his gray eyes flashing. "Why did you make your mother cry?"

I knew Daddy loved me, but Mama was his number one love. Honestly, I had no reply, because I simply did not know.

When a child questions God, it makes a parent fearful—fearful for the child's soul and future. It is very, very hard to put your child into the Lord's hands. I have done so, it seems, at least a thousand times, and then gone back and tried to fix things with my own power and might. I think that might be a book right there for someone.

The Impact of Heartbreak

Around that time, Daddy had tried to get employed again by the Home Mission Board to start another work. He was told they would review his application. They did, however, have an opening for the position of a janitor. Daddy had done all kinds of jobs to bring money in for the family, including a window-washing business with power washers. He was never afraid of hard work. I guess I never thought of him as having an age. He must have been in his mid-forties at the time—not too old, but it was still hard physical work.

We needed to eat, and Daddy had been offered a job, so he went to work each night and cleaned the headquarters building. He was well educated, a Baylor graduate with a degree from Southwestern Theological Seminary, but was also humble and epitomized servanthood. So he did not mind that job at all. I went with Daddy a few times to help, at my request.

After he had been cleaning at night for around a year, Daddy went back to speak to the Home Mission Board executives and asked, "Have you received any word about my request for funding to do another church plant?"

"Oh," they answered back, "that was denied about six months ago." They were so happy with him as a janitor, or perhaps life got too busy, that they forgot to inform him about the denial.

The result was that Daddy's physical heart was now affected by a broken heart. I think he had atrial fibrillation for a while. I did not know at the time just how bad his physical health was, nor the extent of damage to his heart as a result of what he had suffered through pioneering. So I did not realize how horribly this last heartbreak from the denomination he loved affected him. Nor was I aware how much of an impact this event with the Baptists had on me, which would only really be shown to me later in my ministerial life.

Daddy was between churches, and we were struggling. His doctors told him he would die if he did not stop pastoring. In fact, I later learned that he had been given only a year to live if he didn't make a lifestyle change. So after I graduated from

Maryvale High School, my parents moved back to San Antonio, back to our place of oasis and healing, and to my grandmother Lucile McJilton. Mama had also received an inheritance from her uncle, which got us out of deep credit card debt.

During this time, my daddy hid his health struggles from us kids, so we weren't aware how sick he was. His heart was failing, and he looked tired all the time. But he never complained.

Daddy's Unorthodox Innovation

Dad had a degree in teaching, so he got a job at Edison High School teaching shop, which he had also done back in Tolleson, Arizona, when we pioneered in Starlight Park. His methods were rather unorthodox. When kids would become disruptive and break the classroom rules, he had them stand before a court of their peers, who would decide the punishment (within reason, of course). Kids usually straightened up from the sheer humiliation of it. I later used this method when I taught school. The punishments meted out were things like having to clean the classroom, wash all the desks, etc.

Daddy's new job included finding school dropouts and convincing them to come back to high school to attend a special vocation course he had designed for at-risk kids. He personally visited them in their homes and cast a vision of a better future if they would reenroll. Dad's program worked! He made a club out of it, and they all got jackets with patches for each new skill they learned—mechanics, welding, car painting, etc.

The next program he put in place was a first-of-its-kind in Texas. He designed a course that would allow special-needs kids to be mainstreamed into the public school system. He taught them skills that would help them get a job, such as running a cash register, handling interpersonal problems, etc. It was also a huge success. Dad won several awards for the innovative ways he looked at teaching. Again, looking back, I could see he demonstrated to me how to be a problem solver and never take no for an answer when doing the right thing to help people.

5

Falling in Love and Grand Canyon College

I always knew I would go to college one day, and since we were Baptist, my choice of schooling was what was then Grand Canyon College (now University) in Phoenix. Mom and Dad were moving back to San Antonio (again), so I applied for grants and a music scholarship. Between government help, a scholarship for pastors' kids, and a loan, I was able to put together the funds to go to GCC.

For a while I thrived at the school. I auditioned and got into the school's famous choir, The Choralaires, and worked in the dorm for some money for my basic needs. Then, all of a sudden, I just broke.

This time of my life was when the cracks and wounds of our family's spiritual pioneering days were starting to show up in my emotions. I decided that I was going to be a music teacher. My memory of sitting on that big rock at Paradise Valley Ranch and being called of God seemed vague and far off. Children can make emotional decisions, right?! I did not really like many church people. Although I never stopped attending church, I thought the people in our former churches were pretty big hypocrites.

One snapshot of the kind of pain I carried and hid in my emotions was a time when the family went out to eat hamburgers at Bob's Big Boy. The restaurant had incredible hamburgers and wonderful seasoning salt that we put on everything from fries to burgers. We didn't go out that often, so it was a big treat. While we were laughing and eating, a member of a previous church came up to me. With a self-righteous look, she spat out, "You know, our church would have grown so much more if your dad was a better pastor! He never visited people enough or made enough hospital visits!" (This was not Mrs. Leatherberry, but probably a cousin.) I was stunned! Rarely does one have a good comeback in those tense situations. I didn't say much and just turned around and left. Later, I thought, *Maybe if you had helped physically build the building, like Daddy, and sat by bedsides when members were dying, there could have been more visits to well people.*

Life was challenging at best.

Flashbacks and a Crash

I had flashbacks to when I had a very good friend in junior high. We were best buddies, but never boyfriend and girlfriend. I was always over at his house, or he was at mine. We played board games and laughed a lot. As we moved up into higher grades in school, we kind of grew apart, but we were still friends.

One dark night, the phone rang, and my dad answered then left the house. My good friend had been found hanging from a rafter in his family's garage. Dad had been a medic in the Army Air Corps, and he went to be with the family, who lived just up the street from us.

That was another time Dad came home very white and strained. He had tried to revive my friend for some time after cutting him down, but he was dead and could not be revived.

I managed to stuff all my hurt deep inside until my junior year of college. One day, I just broke. The pain inside me crashed in on me, and I got deeply depressed. I called my parents and said I needed to come home.

"I Am the One for You!"

Michael Jacobs and I had fallen in love during that time and were supposed to get married. We had made some beautiful plans, but suddenly, I did not know if I could marry him. I did not really know much of anything anymore.

I'll never forget the night I told Mike, while we were sitting in my gold Buick Riviera, "Mike, I don't know if I love you, or if I want to get married. Don't wait around for me. I release you if you want to be released. You are free to go find someone else."

I am very glad Mike did not take me up on that request. He said, "I am the one for you!" Mike knew and was so certain. That was an anchor for me in my emotional storm.

Frankly, I was a mess! Mom and Dad found me a counselor. I can't say that he did much good. I was obsessed with knowing whether I should marry Mike or not. Every day, I asked God for a sign. The counselor told me he had a son I could meet, and that led me to believe Mike was not the man for me. Of course, after studying psychology, I can see the counselor was way out of bounds.

Faithful Michael would call me often. Those of my generation remember when we paid long-distance charges, and they were expensive. He was working at the railroad in Glendale, Arizona, and must have been spending his salary contacting me! I lived for those calls. When it was time to say good-bye, we would say to each other, "You hang up first!" And the other one would proclaim, "No, you hang up first!" I would wait to see if he hung up first. All the while, the clock was ticking on the call time. Then, I would hear breathing. He was still there! Of course, I really wanted him to still be there.

Mike came to visit me and, to my delight, brought me a puppy. It was a gray-and-white Australian shepherd with one blue eye and one gray eye. He was so much fun! I named him J. Fred Bear. Tigger would have been more appropriate because he bounced around as if he had springs in his feet. God knew I needed solace. My puppy loved Dr Pepper and would follow us around with his bowl in his mouth, begging. (Don't judge us, dog lovers! We didn't know better.)

Recalling the kind of emotional mess I was in, I can't believe Mike stayed the course with me! I could hardly eat, couldn't cry, and was very locked up inside.

Learning That Jesus Bore Our Pain

One day, my daddy sat me down for a talk. Lovingly, he looked at me and said, "Honey, I forgave the church people a long time ago, and you should too. Your unforgiveness is not hurting them, but it is hurting you."

He was right. Of course he was. This began a journey for me of emotional healing. We did not know about inner healing or deliverance yet. I dug into Scripture, and I dug into my heart and soul.

I made list after list. It went far beyond the church members. It included friends, former boyfriends, and me. I took out pictures, wept, and cut some of them up. There were things I had not grieved. I spent time giving those griefs to God.

One Bible verse I love says this: "Surely He has borne our griefs and carried our sorrows; yet we esteemed Him stricken" (Isaiah 53:4). The comments in *The Passion Translation* on Isaiah 53 have this to say about Jesus being stricken: "Jesus was the most emotionally whole and healed man to ever walk the earth. He did not absorb the insults and rejections of even his own neighbors (see Luke 4:14–30)."

Just as Jesus carried and bore our sins on the cross, He also bore our emotional pain.

Another powerful revelation came when I was reading Catherine Marshall's book *Something More.* Catherine wrote how she went through sickness and an emotional crisis. Her story of how she walked out of the valley of despair bolstered me and helped me go deeper with my healing.

I cannot point to one supernatural moment when I got better. Along the way, I was diagnosed with epilepsy and prescribed Dilantin. Of course, I did not have epilepsy! That medication turned my tongue black. I must have suffered something akin to what is called sundown syndrome, because when it started to get dark each night, I fell into a dark, emotional hole. At times, I would lie on my bed and shake. As I worked and worked, however, seeking the Lord for answers, I gradually got a little bit better.

At last, one day the Lord spoke to me that it was time to go back to Phoenix, back to college and Mike. The first thing I did was flush the Valium I had been taking down the toilet. No one told me to do that, and I don't want anyone to do such a thing because I did. I just knew it was the thing to do for me at the time. I called Mike and told him I was coming back and asked if I could stay with his family. His parents graciously said yes, and Mom and Dad bought me a ticket.

I want to parenthetically brag on my mama during this time. Each morning, she would cut a yellow rose from outside our front door and put it in a bud vase by my bed. She would get me little presents and wrap them to cheer me up. Now that I am a parent, I can understand, in a measure, the suffering I put my parents through during my dark night of the soul.

The Journey Toward Victory

Healing from depression was a journey. It was a process. My body was still going through the trauma of the past season. Something Catherine Marshall wrote in *Something More* was that life was to be lived through the truth of the Word of God, not through my emotions. While I had done my homework of forgiving, I still needed healing in my mind and body.

My emotions had been running rampant on me. When I was sick, I would wake up and check with my emotions to see how I was that day. As I was being healed, I would wake up and quote verses from the Bible such as "I can do all things through Christ" (Philippians 4:13). Then I would say, "Body and mind, you are healed by the stripes of Jesus."

Recovery took a while. I started by living at Mike's parents' house. Eventually, I was able to get a job at the teacher's credit union and started saving money. Then, because I needed money for school, I applied for a grant. After being accepted again, I was able to go back to college.

As a music major, I had to choose an instrument, and of course mine was piano. The problem was that my hands were still shaking. One cannot play Chopin with shaking hands. At first, I could play only one key. I recall physically holding my hand with my other hand to help me. After a month or so of this, I found I could start to really practice again. God met me in that little practice room.

In order to be a music major with a concentration in piano, I had to memorize twenty-six pages or so of music from different musical eras, such as baroque and classical. By the end of that semester, I had done that. Mom and Dad flew out to be with me for my junior recital. Before I went up to play, in my beautiful long ecru gown, Daddy said, "Darlin', let me pray with you." He took my small, still-girlish hands in his huge, strong mechanic's ones and earnestly prayed for peace and that God would help me remember my pieces. And I did!

When I started to play, something came over me—a surety, like a blanket. I played under an inspiration I did not know I had! God met me. My grade for the concert from the jury panel was an A. I can still feel the emotional victory of freedom! Victory over fear, intimidation, and depression! While there have been moments when I felt them try to creep back on little cat's feet, I have been able to hold on to that victory, although it would be sorely tested later in my life.

Daddy Was a Bright Light

I am so happy, to this day, that Daddy was there for that performance. Sadly, he was not to live a long life and died a few months later. He was a bright light that made advances and changes for the good of others every day. I was stunned to receive a call from Mama on July 5, 1973, with absolutely shocking news. Daddy was dead.

"Dead?" My brain could not wrap itself around that word! My sister, Lucy, was visiting me, and we had just called him two days before to ask if we could use the credit card to go shopping. He had sounded good, was loving and jovial, and was very much alive. Why, he was only forty-nine years old! It was not possible for him to be dead. He had been going to school in San Marcos, working on continuing education for his school certification. On the side, he worked at a paint and body shop to earn money to pay the family's bills, and he dropped dead on the spot at the shop. He had suffered a massive heart attack and was pronounced dead on arrival.

Grief is a strange thing. It comes and goes in waves. When someone you deeply love passes away, you simply cannot grasp reality. It hits your emotions like a bomb. Daddy was like the glue for the family, the one whom everyone counted on to keep us safe.

Stored in my mind are some very sweet vignettes of the testimonies from his students after he passed away. Mama received letters from former students who had dropped out of school and then had been talked into returning by Daddy. Later, they went on to graduate from college. Daddy had persistently gone after them and encouraged them, telling them they could be somebody, leading to their success.

The owner of the shop where he worked drove from San Marcos to San Antonio for the funeral. His testimony of his relationship with Daddy was like balm to our broken hearts. He shared how one day he had offered Daddy a cold beer to quench his thirst. Daddy simply said, "Oh, no thank you!"

Later, this man found out Daddy was a Southern Baptist pastor. I will never forget the look on the man's face as he relayed this story to my sister and me. Everyone in Texas, at least then, knew that offering a beer to a Southern Baptist pastor, no matter how hot the day, was a big no-no!

He stopped a moment, gathering himself, and got out the words, "I went to him the next day and said, 'Pastor, I am so sorry! Did I offend you?'" Moving on with the story, the man said, "I can't believe how your daddy answered me! He looked at me and, with the kindest voice, said, 'Oh, I hope I didn't hurt your feelings!'"

One sentence uttered with sweetness and a lack of condemnation can change a life. That owner saw a side of a Christ-filled pastor he had never before experienced. What did I learn? It is God's kindness that leads us to repentance. It was like Jesus telling Zacchaeus, "Come down from the tree; I am going to stay at your house" (see Luke 19:1–10). He did not tell Zacchaeus what a bad man he was; He validated him to be worthy of a rabbi staying with him. He knew Zacchaeus was wicked and corrupt, but the love Jesus offered transformed him.

After we buried Daddy, we had lots of decisions to make and things to do to wrap up his estate. Dad had tools stashed all over the city, as well as cars he had purchased to fix up for extra money for the family. While he was a good provider, he was terrible at keeping a checkbook and stored the car titles and other important documents all over the place.

Mike to the Rescue

Mike came to the rescue. Even though we were officially not a couple at the time, he bought a ticket and flew to San Antonio to help us. My daddy loved Mike. He wrote me a letter when I lived in Phoenix, sharing with me what a good man Mike was and what a good husband he would be. His actions began to overcome my fears.

I was pretty hard-headed, though. One time when I had been in San Antonio, I told my mom and grandmother, "I do not want to marry Mike just because everyone loves him." Add stubbornness to the list of things God needed to break in me. Later, that has mostly been turned to tenacity and endurance, but I can still be stubborn at times. (I did not realize that writing one's memoirs would be a "tell all your faults" situation!)

Mike knew about tools, and he knew about fixing things. I realize that was one of the many appealing things about him. (Not to mention his gorgeous good looks and muscles!) He was also intelligent. I could never abide a dumb man.

All this was leading up to the next phase of my life. I just did not know it yet.

6

Wedding Bells and California

After Daddy died, I had a choice to make. Would I go back to Phoenix, where Mike was, and back to Grand Canyon College, or not? I was not in a good place, and I wasn't sure how I would survive financially. Miss Clarice Maben, a history professor at my school, had offered me a place to stay with her for fifteen dollars a month. I realized later it was awfully generous even for that time. Prices were vastly different from now, though. Gasoline cost fifteen cents a gallon. A good wage was one or two dollars an hour. I had started working as a bank teller at the Desert Schools Federal Credit Union while staying with the Jacobses. As a result, I could pay the fifteen dollars.

After a few months, I applied for a music scholarship from Grand Canyon, and with grant money, had my school year paid. I went back. Mama gave me a bit of money to help me get started, and I worked part-time at the credit union. Thankfully, I had a car that Daddy had bought, repaired, and painted for me. Daddy died just before my twentieth birthday, and I had to grow up.

Mike was there for me, even though I broke up with him multiple times.

I enjoyed living with Miss Maben, although she had to give me a serious talking-to about helping around the house. I am embarrassed to think how totally unaware I was that I needed to help. After that, I tried to make up for lost time!

Love Casts Out Fear

Mike graduated from Arizona State University with a degree in business administration. He had also studied prelaw, which has come in handy with the ministry we have today, Generals International. In addition, he studied transportation and had a desire to work for the airlines. He went out to Los Angeles with the father of a friend and walked around asking agents at the ticket counters about working for their airline. He got an interview with Trans World Airlines (TWA, now defunct). They were reluctant to hire him because the only opening they had was washing dishes in the kitchen. (Those were the days when they used real dishes and fed even economy class on an airplane.) He convinced them he wanted the job, and they hired him. He worked his way up to making salads, until he eventually got a job loading bags onto the planes. Finally, he was hired as a manager and was able to use his college degree in business management.

I was shocked Mike was going to leave Phoenix! How could that be? I had a full-ride music scholarship for my senior year and wanted to finish school. After he moved to El Segundo, California, right next to the LA airport, I missed him desperately. I was torn as to what to do and still afraid of commitment. Frankly, I didn't think I could love any guy for the rest of my life! What if I failed?

By that time, Mike had decided he did not want a long-distance relationship and we would have to break up if I didn't marry him, and he told me so. I thought, *Well, that is awfully audacious!* I knew I missed him, and by then I had come to the realization that I could not do life without him.

Not doing life without Mike meant giving up my scholarship. It was a leap of faith for me. It was also a leap of faith for Mike, as I had not been able to make up my mind!

I called him in Los Angeles and told him, "Mike, if the offer is still good, I want to get married."

He said he had been praying about what we should do and reading Matthew 18:19: "Again I say to you that if two of you agree on earth concerning anything that they ask, it will be done for them by My Father in heaven."

Mike agreed to fly out that Wednesday, his next day off, and we would go hunting for a ring. When we looked at our schedules, he would not get time off again for three months, and I would need to go to school if we didn't marry right away. We decided to get married that next week, as school was starting soon.

When we looked at rings, I froze. That fear gripped me again! Finally, I began remembering the Scripture "There is no fear in love; but perfect love casts out fear, because fear involves torment. But he who fears has not been made perfect in love" (1 John 4:18). I knew I loved Mike, and I needed to trust God and not give in to fear.

We finally did buy two wedding rings. No diamonds. They were way too expensive for us. (I would wear that single band until our twenty-fifth wedding anniversary, when a jeweler we met in Guatemala, who had made rings for other ministry leaders, designed one commissioned by Mike for me.) I was almost twenty-two and Mike was twenty-five when we got married. (Yes, I married an older man!)

A Simple Start

Our ceremony was simple. Mom was the only family member there. She rushed to the airport with my wedding veil, made the ticket counter open up, purchased a ticket, and caught the last flight out of San Antonio. (My brother was in China at the time, and my sister was in Minneapolis.) She was quite an amazing mom!

Miss Maben arranged flowers from her garden, and we married in her living room. The pastor who married us was a friend of my dad's who ran the Baptist Children's Home. I wore the dress my daddy had seen me in at my junior recital, and the veil my mom brought, which I had previously purchased.

Mike thought I might have skipped out the back because Miss Maben told me to wait until after she had played about half of the wedding march. He said he was thinking, *If she skipped out the back, our relationship is over!* But I didn't! The wedding ceremony was sweet, and we were duly bound together by God.

After the morning wedding and lunch, Mike and I started packing up our possessions in a U-Haul trailer to head to California. My books took up three-quarters of it, and he had only a few boxes. In our life today, that would probably still be the case! Of course, if we were talking about tools, he would far outstrip me. The testimony for that is in our garage.

We drove about forty-five minutes out of our way to spend our wedding night at a beautiful resort in Cave Creek, Arizona. It was a short night because we didn't have our wedding dinner until ten p.m., and we had to leave again for Los Angeles at four the next morning. Bright and early, we started our trek across the desert to Los Angeles because Mike had to go to work the next morning. The air conditioner was not working, so I sat with a chunk of ice in a basin in front of me to try to keep things bearable.

When we got to El Segundo, a beachside town in Los Angeles County that would be our first home, the car died. We found that the car's engine had severe problems and never should have worked going across that desert. God had supernaturally met us going across that barren land.

7

El Segundo and Pepperdine University

We found a little apartment that was up on the second floor over a garage. It was tiny. We had only a three-quarter bed, and I had to move my bicycle to get into the fridge and Mike's bicycle to get into our chest of drawers. But together, we made it into our newlywed home.

Mike bought a car for two hundred dollars that was a mess. The hatchback was caved in and was held down with a bungee cord. Even though the car looked awful, we were ecstatic! We wouldn't have to get groceries from the 7-Eleven next door.

Mike had to work nights. He took a big black lunch box to work, and I made him multiple sandwiches to put inside. Eating out was relegated to celebrations. Despite the challenges, we enjoyed our newly married life together, although our peace was sometimes disturbed by the people next door, who would fight at night. It was loud and scary.

The school year had already started in California, and I knew I would need a scholarship, so I stayed home that first year. This was a lonely time. We had a red phone and a landline, but I didn't know anyone to call—not a soul! Long-distance calling was too expensive and could only be done maybe once a week. There was only snail mail to communicate. I will never forget Mike reading my mom's long, newsy letters out loud. I would find out later that he interjected his own lines, like "How is that handsome and wonderful husband of yours?" A sweet memory now.

To get to work at the Los Angeles International Airport, Mike rode his bicycle on back roads at midnight, with only a small bike light to see by and be seen. One night, a buddy from work saw him and started driving him to and fro every day. What a relief!

Not a Long Shot with God

I went to Pepperdine University to try out for a music scholarship. It is a Christian school, and I felt they would take my credits from Grand Canyon College. Pepperdine is and was one of the more expensive schools in the United States, and it was a long shot to try, but not with God.

I got a full-ride scholarship at Pepperdine in exchange for playing the piano for the chorale's practices. I loved studying with Hansel Rayner, the conductor for the Burbank Symphony. He was my piano teacher and instructor. To this day, I have fond memories of sitting as a one-person audience, observing his conducting style at the practice for the Burbank Symphony. Music was my passion!

During my student-teaching semester in a junior high school, I also found out I loved to teach. The students were so dear to me, although one did raise his hand and asked me out in the middle of class. I looked much younger than twenty-three. This happened when I taught seventh and eighth grade later as well.

"Are You Feeling More Fatherly?"

After Mike and I had been married around four years, we started discussing children. I distinctly recall saying to him at our little dinner table, "Are you feeling more fatherly lately?"

To which he questioned me too: "Why? Are you feeling more motherly?"

It was about three months later that we were pregnant with our daughter, Mary. While pregnant, I went to California State University, Dominguez Hills, to do additional coursework. I would play my guitar with the sound reverberating into my belly, and our daughter is musical today.

I had a hard time giving birth. My heart rate was dropping, and so was Mary's. Finally, the doctors rushed me to the operating room for an emergency C-section. C-sections in those days were very painful, more than today with the newer techniques. But we were parents!

Graduation and a Graduate Fellowship

I finally graduated in 1975 with a degree in music education and wanted to start my fifth year in a master of arts program for teaching music. Again, we didn't have any money, so I asked to see if I could get a graduate fellowship, as my grades were excellent. I was turned down! There was no money. A week later, as I was praying, I felt the Lord nudge me to ask again. This time, they had just received an endowment, and I was granted a full graduate fellowship.

I got a teaching position in El Segundo after we had Mary, and a friend kept her while I taught. This helped us tremendously in paying back the money we had borrowed from friends to get into our first house. I taught music in two elementary schools. It was mostly fun, except for the end of the sixth-grade year, when the kids thought they were too grown-up for music.

We moved to Inglewood, and the drive to school was around half an hour each way. A friend who lived just down the street from the school offered day care for a very affordable fee, and Mary loved the attention from that family's girls.

We bought our first house in Inglewood. It was tiny but had a big garden in the back, and we loved it! I started gardening and still enjoy it to this day. Plants make me happy!

One day, Mike came home to say he had been laid off from his job. We had just a little money, a small child, and no family that could help us out financially. But we knew how to have faith. We prayed and believed God and tightened our belts. I bought a huge turkey for eighteen cents a pound and made every turkey dish one could imagine.

One night, our doorbell sounded, and it was a friend of Mike's. He had a check in his hand for what in those days was a very substantial amount of money! It turned out that we gave half of it away to help some Iranian friends who had gotten stuck in the United States without funds while they were attending school. Later, one of those men got saved, so it was well worth the sacrifice! When Mike finally got another job, we still had around two hundred dollars in savings after several months of no work, and to this day, I can't tell you how.

From Slow to Lightning Speed

Around that time, Mike had been feeling that we were going to move back to Texas, and I was too. But we had not shared that with each other. Little did we know that we had both thought

Dallas or San Antonio. We would make it to Texas, but just barely so, geographically.

We went to see his parents in Phoenix for Christmas. We had driven our beat-up car across the desert a number of times, only this time it broke down. Mike had to walk to the nearest town while Mary and I waited, at night, in the car. His dad came and rescued us. We were about halfway there.

On the way home, we started to worship the Lord, and did so most of the way to LA. I believe that worship brought our breakthrough. The next morning, the phone rang early. It was the manager for the American Airlines station in El Paso, Texas. He was offering Mike a job. When Mike asked when it would start, he replied, "After New Year's."

That was only a few days away. Have you ever noticed how things seem to be so slow with God, and then He goes into fast-forward?

When Mike was first laid off, we believed he would have a job by October 15 and prayed for that, but it didn't seemingly happen. Now it was the end of December. When Mike asked him how he got his application, the manager said, "Oh, the LA employment office forwarded it to me." The job had been open since October, and they had been looking all that time for the right person to hire. Somehow, his application got bounced around from station to station until God saw that it got to Texas.

The other special thing that happened around that time was an answer to prayer as well. I had believed I would get to go see my mom for Christmas. Christmas came, and we had no money, so I went to Phoenix. Mike's mom at that time had said to me when I shared this with her, "Well, I guess God was out of Christmas miracles!" Ouch! She later got filled with the Holy Spirit and greatly softened. When we got back home, the neighbors brought our mail over, and there was a check in the mail with plenty of money for a ticket home to San Antonio to see my mom and stepdad. God is good! He wasn't out of Christmas miracles!

Things then moved at lightning speed. Mike flew to El Paso, was hired, and went to work. I stayed home in Inglewood to sell the house. The sale took a few months, but then we were back in Texas again, just barely! We loved it, though.

8

The Dark Night of the Soul and Great Joy

Have you noticed that God does not waste anything? Some of my toughest times hardened me to adversities while also giving me compassion for those who suffer. The Lord had opened the door to El Paso, and we were about to enter graduate school in learning how to pray, hear God's voice, and navigate deep waters.

Mike and I went house shopping and found a lovely old craftsman-style home in the historic Five Points area. It was one of those homes that we say "has good bones," meaning it had lovely features and was solidly built, but needed so much work.

At that juncture, what did that matter? The house had 1920s plaster moldings with beautiful flowers, enormous windows, twelve-inch-thick walls on the bottom floor, and ten-inch-thick walls on the top floor. It had expansive twelve-foot ceilings and hardwood floors. The staircase in the foyer made two turns and swept up beyond view.

I am not sure how much we really interceded about buying that house. If we had known American Airlines was going to go through a consolidation and, only six months after we moved, transfer Mike to the headquarters in Dallas, we would have at least thought twice.

Nevertheless, we rolled up our sleeves. Mike started sanding and restoring the floors. I took charge of remodeling the kitchen, and we took out a wall. Lath and plaster walls are a mess to remove!

We had moved into a mostly Latino neighborhood, and we loved it. The church we attended was pastored by a great group of men. It was two churches that had merged. We jumped in with both feet and started a home group.

One night, one of the pastors from the church came to our meeting. I didn't know why at the time, but he and some of the leadership had decided I had demons because of my prophetic gift. One of the main ones was spiritual pride. They asked if Mike and I would sit in chairs, as they wanted to pray for us. They proceeded to attempt deliverance on me. Finally, Mike said, "Cut it out! This isn't right!" If I had had spiritual pride, it was well pulverized at that moment.

We probably should have left that church, but we had made friends in the congregation, so we stayed. Mike and I had doubled our money on our house in Los Angeles, and we began to make anonymous gifts to members of the congregation. It was so much fun! If a need was announced, we would go to the church office and sow. One family had a fire, and we loved the testimony of their rebuilding and incredulous joy at not knowing from where the money was supplied.

The Daniel Dream

When we were still living in Los Angeles, Mike had a dream that we had a son, and that we were to call him Daniel. This was so unlike my husband at the time that, when he awakened me to tell me what happened, I looked at him askance and thought, *What alien has stolen my husband's body?*

Mike was simply not given to doing that sort of thing. He was Mr. Analyst! I sometimes called him Mr. Spock (the Vulcan from the television series *Star Trek*).

Both of us knew, however, that it was a dream from God. One day, after we moved to El Paso, we discussed that dream again. Mary was two and a half, and both of us felt like it was time for Daniel to come into our lives. I loved being with our daughter, and we had sweet times together, but it was time for us to build on our family.

Believing God speaks through dreams doesn't seem unusual to you if you are used to having dreams and visions. But for us at the time, we were very new to charismatic-type expressions. We were learning. The dream was just so real to us that we never questioned it.

One special night, Mike read different places in the Word where God had promised a child to a couple. We knelt down and made sure we forgave each other for anything we might have held against each other, and then Mike prayed for our son, Daniel.

We found out one month later that I got pregnant that night. This was all right before Mike's transfer. When the doctor told us we were going to have a baby, we were absolutely elated. This was it! Our son was coming!

I realize now that God sometimes gives such a strong prophecy before an event because it is one we will need to cling to. We did not know about 1 Timothy 1:18, which says, “This charge I commit to you, son Timothy, according to the prophecies previously made concerning you, that by them you may wage the good warfare.” The war was on for our son’s life. We just didn’t know it yet.

Mike proudly told his colleagues at American Airlines we were pregnant and were having a son named Daniel. They thought he had lost his mind. Bets were made and odds calculated whether we would have a boy or girl. Friendly advice was given, as in, “Well, if you do have a girl, you will still love her, right?”

A Crisis of Faith and a Commitment

Then, right in the middle of the pregnancy, Mike was transferred to the company’s headquarters in Dallas. American Airlines would fly him out Monday mornings around five to get him to work on time. I was left alone with our three-year-old daughter, feeling very lonely and overwhelmed. Our air-conditioning broke in the midst of 103-degree weather. We sweated out each night with fans. Mike finally got home and installed coolers, and life got much, much better.

Both of us thought we would put the house on the market and it would sell quickly, and we would be together again. Right? Wrong! Our beautiful house did not sell. Month after month went by, and I grew bigger and bigger with Daniel. I “extended my faith” and declared we would be together in Dallas before the baby was born. When month seven rolled around, that dream died. I was devastated.

It also seemed that our friends had kind of forgotten us. I went weeks without seeing anyone, except when Mike could get home on a Friday night, only to leave again early Monday morning.

I found a Bible study near our house at a church called Abundant Living Center. They taught the Word, and we loved it. Each week, I faithfully took Mary, and we went and learned more about the Holy Spirit.

Being a "single mother" during the week was a challenge. Our little blond-haired wonder was going through a challenging season. One day at the Bible study, I heard someone shout out loud, "Whose child is this?"

I didn't have to turn to know whose it was, even though I wanted to say, "I don't know! What mother let that child run around like that?!"

It was Mary. She had gone to the bookstore and spun around a display of minibooks, and now they all lay scattered on the floor. Thank God for the ladies who helped the pregnant lady pick up all those books!

In my eighth month of pregnancy, I had a crisis of faith. I couldn't seem to hear God's voice anymore. In the past, we just walked and talked, and now He seemed silent—very, very silent. I would pray and beg God to tell me something about my situation. *Lord*, I would pray, *when is our house going to sell*? The quiet was deafening.

One cold, blustery night, I made my way down the stairs and stood in our now-restored living room. I held my Bible in my hands and lifted it up in the air—just me, God, and the angels. This was my prayer: *Lord, if You never speak to me again, except through Your Word, I know the Bible is true. I will serve You to my dying day. All my life is Yours, and I will never turn back.*

Digging In to the Scriptures

I call this season my dark night of the soul. I was so used to just asking and hearing right away. Part of my training was that I needed to know the Scriptures, and I needed to know them well.

So I dug in!

I also learned to pray the Word. My friend Germaine Copeland had just written her book *Prayers That Avail Much*. It was full of Scripture. Remember, this was the 1980s. Scripture praying was just really gaining ground as an intercessory emphasis. I learned from that book. I prayed over the baby, Mike, our daughter, the house, nations, my friends, and the church. The Word started to live in me. I ate it for my daily bread. As I write this, I just gave an endorsement for the forty-year anniversary of that book. Germaine, thank you for writing it, if only for me!

Mike's mom, Helen, flew out to be with me the last couple of weeks of my pregnancy. We had a great time, and she was a big help. My mom had a job, so she could not come at that time.

The Very, Very Long Night

One day, I thought my amniotic fluid was leaking. I went to the doctor, and I was so excited. Most of my friends were having their babies at home, and the physician had said I should try to have this baby naturally. Helen and I went to the hospital, and we called Mike. By God's grace, he was able to arrive before the birth.

With today's medical advancements, one can tell the sex of a child before the birth. In those days, sonograms were grainy at best, and we weren't sure. Anticipation was mounting, both with us and the people who had made bets at American Airlines.

After being admitted, I could tell something was wrong. I was hot, flushed, and running a fever. The tear in my amniotic sac had allowed an infection to set in. The baby was in danger, and so was I. They prepped me for surgery. I started to cry. This was not right! I wanted a natural birth.

Mike scrubbed up to go into the operating room with me. Soon, I heard a cry and knew the child of promise had been born. The doctor held him up for me so see. I noticed three things right away: He was blue, he had a foot that looked like it was crushed, and I was in a lot of pain!

The wonderful news was that our Daniel was born. The challenging news was that he was very sick. They rushed him to ICU as I lay in recovery.

That was a very, very long night. I lay in that single bed in the hospital room and stared at the ceiling. I kept crying out to God to heal Daniel. Every time nurses came to check on my condition, they would only tell me, "He is holding his own."

The next day, the doctor gave us the full report. Daniel had a blood condition that caused his red blood cells not to reproduce. They were giving him blood transfusions to help sustain him, but he was not self-sustaining.

I felt ashamed. I thought I must not have had enough faith for a natural delivery. It seemed to me that was the reason no one came to see me in the hospital. I was thankful that, after three days, a pastor came and prayed with me.

My mom came, Mike's mom was still there, and a friend of ours took Mary. Daniel was small (not even seven pounds) and a bit premature. He had tubes coming into his chest and head, and he was in an incubator. We found out he had what is called a club foot on the same side my mother had one. She always wore two different sizes of shoes because of it. Mom felt guilty. She knew it wasn't her fault, yet somehow she felt like it was.

God healed Daniel's blood condition by the morning after his birth. He was still in a very delicate condition, but he would live.

Later, I realized that at Calvary, God gave our baby His blood for his healing. I felt so grateful.

When they put Daniel in my arms at last, the joy in my heart was huge! He was worth all the suffering, all the pain, everything a mother goes through to have a child.

I had to leave Daniel in the hospital for about ten more days after I went home. Mike had to go back to work, our moms went home, and it was just Mary and me. We lived in a two-story house and did not have any help. It was so hard, having had an extreme C-section, to get up and down those stairs. I had to carry the baby and make sure Mary did not do anything life-threatening to herself. I recall going up those stairs one time murmuring to God, "Lord, You say that You will not give us more than we can bear, but there is a decided difference of opinion of what I can stand!"

Storming Heaven for Daniel

The doctor referred us to a specialist to have Daniel's club foot condition checked out and see what we could do to fix it. The specialist said we needed to put it in a cast while it was still malleable. Once a month, I would have to soak off the cast because the doctor did not want to cut it off. Daniel did not like having to be still and having his cast soaked. Sometimes he would cry, and I would just cry with him. His big sister stood on a stool by the sink and "helped."

When Daniel was ten months old, I took him to the pediatrician for a check-up. I had noticed Daniel did not try to pull up in his crib, and he couldn't really crawl. I had thought it was because of his cast, but when the doctor tested his leg to check his reflexes, he looked at me with a sober face and said, "He does not seem to have reflexes in his left leg, as well as the club foot.

I am not sure he will be able to walk, because he does not have the muscle tone to do so."

I was deeply distressed. Mike was at work in Dallas, and I recall putting Daniel in his car seat, driving home, and trying to pray. Thank God for prayer partners and for Mike. We started storming heaven for him. My friend said she had a vision of Daniel playing baseball and running. I clung to that vision!

Every day, I would hold his foot in my hands and pray over his leg and say over him, "Daniel, you're going to walk. You're going to run and not be weary and walk and not faint!" This went on for months, but there was no change. At last, when he was about a year old, he pulled himself up in the crib, but he still could not walk.

"Look Up!"

During this season, I began to study the gifts of the Holy Spirit. Little by little, I started practicing moving in the power of God. This included the gift of tongues and interpretation. One Sunday morning, I felt a heavy presence of God upon me. At first, I surmised this must be God wanting me to give a word in tongues. That wasn't hard, right? The problem was that I needed to stand up and actually open up my mouth. The presence did not lift, so I stood up and gave a word in tongues.

Then I waited. I had done my part, right? Now, surely, one of the more spiritual people in the crowd would interpret. The seconds ticked by and nothing happened. Mike told me later that he was praying and praying, begging God to tell me what had been prophesied.

Suddenly, I knew what I had to do. I had to get over my shyness completely and trust the Holy Spirit to give me the interpretation. So I did! It is etched in my heart and mind today. It went like this:

> When you cannot see the way to go, and everywhere you look around you is walled, look up! I have the answers. I will not leave you or forsake you in your time of crisis. I will reach My hand down to you and pull you up out of your box and save you.

Great word, even for today! I was elated, and something definitely broke inside of me. I had allowed the Holy Spirit to have control of what I said and when I said it. Bondages came off me that day. Yes, I must admit that I sat down shaken and relieved. The pastor smiled and acknowledged they received the word. And really, the rest is part of my history. It was quite a beginning.

This released the power of God inside me on a new level. The next Wednesday night, when I stepped into the building, it seemed like a mantle fell on my shoulders. I prophesied to everyone I saw. People were falling under the power and weeping! Wow, God is so dramatic!

One of the most encouraging prophecies I received during that time actually came from my three-year-old daughter while she was hooked into her car seat. Suddenly, she proclaimed, "Mommy, everything is going to be okay." I lived on that word!

Three a.m. Wake-Up Calls

Mike was living with some family friends of ours from Weatherford, a city about an hour away from the airport, as we could not afford two house payments. This temporary situation went on for almost a year.

One dark morning at three o'clock, when Mike was getting ready to fly back to El Paso, I begged him not to go. It was only a short while after my C-section, and I told him I could not stand any more of being alone and taking care of the kids while still recovering from surgery. He reluctantly left anyway because he had to keep his job. After Mike was gone, I got very real with God. "God," I said emphatically, "I don't believe that You love me. If You loved me, all these bad things would not be happening." With that, I fell asleep.

The next morning, the phone rang. It was Mike's cousin, who lived in California. We had not seen him in about five years. He said, "Cindy, are you all right? The Lord awakened me at three a.m. with you on my heart, and I felt compelled to call you."

Three a.m.! That was exactly the time I had had my meltdown. As wonderful as that was, the Lord wasn't finished comforting me yet. A few hours later, the phone rang again. This time it was the father of a girl with whom I had gone to Grand Canyon College. He was a good friend of Mike's parents. I was astounded both by the fact that he called and by what he said: "Cindy, I awakened at three a.m. and felt that I just had to get your number from your folks, and call and tell you that God loves you." I thanked him and sat down, awed by the two calls.

Later that day, the doorbell rang. I opened the door and saw a woman I did not know. She explained she was the church secretary for the pastor at Abundant Living Center. Her next words are ones I can still feel deep in my heart today: "Cindy, you don't know me, but in the night at three a.m., I was compelled to go to church, find your address, and come to your house with a message from the Lord." God told her to find me and tell me that He really loved me. To say that action changed my life would be a gross understatement.

It is one thing to mentally acquiesce that God loves us, as the Bible tells us so. One of the first Bible verses we learn as children is John 3:16. God is love. However, it is another thing to know it. God loves us, and He specifically loves you. After that day, I knew that I knew that He loved me. That fact has sustained me through some rough patches of persecution, loneliness, despair, rejection, and challenges in faith.

The house sold at last, and we were on the way to Weatherford, Texas, which was the beginning of our ministry and big open doors. Daniel turned one the day after we made the move. The dark night of the soul was about to get brighter.

9

Juggling Being a Mommy and a Minister

When we moved from El Paso, it would make sense for us to live near the Dallas Fort Worth International Airport. Mike had a management job at the headquarters there, and living close would be best, right? We did look around a bit near DFW but just did not feel at home. Besides, our friends Hayseed and Mary Gene Stephens lived near Weatherford, a small town with a population of twelve thousand at the time.

Weatherford is a beautiful town. It is full of Victorian houses and good people. One of our favorite places to go was the farmers market for their scrumptious peaches. There was also a large flea market event each month where people brought their goods to sell. It was called First Monday because it took place the weekend before the first Monday of the month. It was originally tied to the farmers bringing their produce to market, but it had grown beyond simply selling fruit and vegetables to become a large event. Farmers also brought their livestock (such as baby pigs), and it served as a petting zoo for our kids. Best of all, it was free, and our family loved going!

The Fixer-Upper

The economy in 1981 was in rough shape, and mortgage interest rates had skyrocketed to 16 percent. We had some money from the sale of our previous home, but we didn't want to spend it all; we wanted to reserve some to give away. So we bought a fixer-upper.

The house sat on a corner lot. It was made of wood and was probably built around 1947. It was about 1,900 square feet, and it needed work—a *lot* of work. Keep in mind, we had just poured sweat equity into our house in El Paso, and now here we were, starting all over again. To this day, Mike says his palms sweat when he walks through a fixer-upper!

I walked through that house calling out changes: "We need to move that wall, open up that space, and add some architectural detail to the front porch." Here's a little secret—I've always loved interior design. From the time I was young, I would check out books from the library about furniture, color palettes, and creative use of space. Thankfully, Mike and I have very similar tastes—what I would call "traditionally elegant."

The house had no insulation and needed all-new drywall. It was freezing in the winter and sweltering in the summer. One contractor we hired moved our front room walls out without installing weight-bearing beams to support the roof. When we came home and saw the roof sagging, we realized the damage—and the danger.

Eventually, we ran out of money to keep going. We had given it all away. I remember one day I was complaining to the Lord that I didn't even have the money to put new flooring in the living room. The existing floor was a mix of subfloor plywood, wood slats, and remnants from what used to be the front porch. As I poured out my frustrations to God, I felt the Holy Spirit check me. I heard Him say, very clearly: *Cindy, did you ask Me if you should give away the money you had for the house?*

I was stunned into silence. Then He continued, *I've given you the money for that floor three times—and each time, you gave it away. Now, the next time I provide for that flooring, use it for the floor.*

It was a gentle but firm correction. That moment was a turning point for me. When you carry a gift of giving, you also must learn when to give and when not to. For us, it has always been easier to give than to hold back.

In another instance, we had loaned what was, for us, a large amount of money to someone. Not only did he fail to repay it, but he never even mentioned it again. At one point, this man had even promised Mike a very high-paying job and told me I'd have carte blanche to fund other ministries. It all sounded very exciting for a couple in their thirties.

This man was involved in international business, and the promise was always, "The money is coming in next week." But it never did. We eventually chose to forgive him. It was a painful experience, but it taught us a lasting lesson about stewarding the gift of giving—a lesson that still serves us well today.

Watching Daniel's Miracle Unfold

During our time in Weatherford, we were deeply involved with Living Way Church. As I mentioned in the last chapter, my

Sundays were full—leading worship, training the worship team, slipping out to teach the children's church, then slipping back in to help close the service. Sundays were nonstop.

At the same time, we were still contending for Daniel's healing. We continued declaring Isaiah 40:31 over him: "[He] shall run and not be weary, [he] shall walk and not faint." We started proclaiming that promise when he was just ten months old. But months passed—eleven, twelve, thirteen—and still, he could not walk.

Then, one Wednesday night when Daniel was almost seventeen months old, something miraculous happened. We were at church, and I watched him pull himself up using the chairs and—right there in the sanctuary—he walked down the aisle!

I stood transfixed, watching this long-awaited miracle unfold. From that night on, he never looked back. He ran, played Little League baseball, swam, and enjoyed all the things little boys love. Thank You, Lord!

A Defining Lesson About Demons

One of the most defining spiritual lessons I learned in this season was how to cast out demons. Although the Bible commands us to do it, no one had ever taught me how. But the Holy Spirit had a way of pushing me into learning—ready or not!

We had invited Lois, a woman who was going through a very difficult time, to stay with us. One day, she suddenly manifested a demon. In a low, eerie, masculine voice she said, "I'm going to kill myself."

I was terrified—not just for her, but for my young children, who were also in the house. Her entire demeanor had changed—like someone else had taken over her body. Lois was also, naturally, much bigger than me. I somehow convinced her to lie down, thinking that might help. (Looking back, I can't imagine why I thought that would make a difference!) In that same man's voice, she kept saying, "Her family murdered people down a well, and now I'm going to kill her for it."

I jumped on the bed, trying to restrain her. I had no idea what I was doing, but I just kept saying, "In the name of Jesus, you will not harm her or anyone else. I bind you in Jesus' name."

Eventually, the spirit left, and the woman returned to her normal voice. Later, she sought deliverance with a team more experienced than I was at the time—and I heard she threw several grown men across the room during her session! When I told Mike what had happened, he said, "Honey, I forbid you to cast out demons. You could get hurt!" We were both on a steep learning curve.

That year, I was invited to attend a deliverance seminar with Vinita Copeland. Mike and I had already been learning from *Pigs in the Parlor: A Practical Guide to Deliverance* by Frank and Ida Mae Hammond, who later became our friends. The seminar was a practicum where we watched live deliverances. During one session, a demon-possessed person looked at me and said, "I know you."

Something in me rose up, and I shot back, "You better believe you do—and I command you in the name of Jesus to come out!"

The spirit left immediately. Vinita leaned over and whispered, "That was one of the cleanest deliverances I've seen. You're called to cast out demons."

We went to watch another deliverance taking place, and the man started speaking in a foreign language he did not know how to speak. He then began wringing his hands together, saying in English, "I was there with the pigs. . . . I was there with the pigs."

We easily understood that he was talking about when Jesus cast Legion out of the man of the Gadarenes.

I was exhausted when I got home that night. The next day, a friend called me and asked what I was doing. I told her, "I'm in bed with the sheets over my head, and I have stapled them shut and am not coming out!"

She said, "Well, Cindy, why?"

I moaned, "Vinita Copeland says that I am called to cast out demons, and I don't want anything more to do with demons!"

Of course, you know that I did get out of bed, and I have since cast out many, many demons. I got over myself.

A Really Big Angel

Weatherford was my Holy Spirit training ground. I devoured books on the supernatural, listened to tapes of Derek Prince's teachings on spiritual warfare, and practiced what I read. At the time, I really felt like I was doing everything I could to serve the Lord. People would fly in to see us, and Mike and I would get a babysitter and minister to these people. We never charged anyone. He was working full-time at American Airlines, and we were blessed.

It is interesting how God can utterly disrupt our notion of what we should be doing with our lives, though. Our lives were about to get rocked in a big way!

One night, I was up washing dishes while the rest of the family was asleep. The way our house was laid out, one could look from the kitchen through a swinging door to the dining room and all the way into the living room. As I was drying my hands, I felt something I had never experienced before—it was like the glory of God was in our front room!

I walked through the dining room, and to my shock, a big angel was sitting in a very tall, blue velvet chair in the living room. Many people ask me, "Cindy, how did you know it was an angel?" All I can say is that you know; you just know.

What did I do? I fell on my face on the floor! It is not uncommon for this to occur, as we've seen this happen in the Bible when people saw angels. What did he look like? He was big—really big. His shoulders were way over the top of the wing-backed chair. He had a crown across his forehead and wore a brilliant white robe, a gold sash, and sandals. The most astonishing things were his eyes. They looked deep into mine, and all I felt was such love—while I knew he could see deep down into my very soul. I thought, *It's the Lord!*

Reading my thoughts, he said to me, "I am not the Lord, but I am the angel of the Lord. Rise on your feet!"

I did as he said. In the next moments, he showed me that I would go to the whole world and minister. I cannot explain more about that, but in the next few days I would get more revelation. At the end, he said, "Go call Lois, and she will explain more about what you have seen." (Remember, Lois was the lady from whom I tried to cast out the demon. By this time she had been delivered for a while, and we had gotten to know each other better.)

It was now ten thirty, which was pretty late to call someone. But after that encounter, I did not hesitate. I explained to my friend what had happened. She got quiet and then said, "Cindy, I have seen that same angel."

She went on to describe how, as a child, she contracted polio and was dying. There were no polio vaccines then, and that disease killed many children. She was in the hospital in what they called an iron lung—a full-body breathing machine.

"One night," she went on to say, "I opened my eyes, and there was an angel floating at the end of the iron lung. He floated up and right above the iron lung. I will never forget what he looked like. He wore a crown across his forehead, just as you described. I went to sleep immediately, and when I woke up, I was completely healed."

I hung up the phone, stunned. Since I didn't know what to do, I decided to wake Mike up to help me figure it out. It was around midnight by that time, and I knew he had to get up early. But I needed help! I gently shook him awake and tried to talk to him. To my shock, I could not speak in English—I could only speak in tongues! Now, this was scary! What had happened to me?

Mike looked at me and murmured, "I cannot understand a thing you're saying." He then proceeded to roll over and go back to sleep. Sleeping! What in the world was he doing going back to sleep? I realize now that he probably was not fully awake. So I did what any wife would do under those circumstances—when she was lost in some spiritual place she did not understand and worried she would never speak English again—I shook him awake more firmly!

"Michael," I urged, "you have got to wake up now and do something!"

Of course, I did not say that in English either, but he got the drift. He pointed to me and said, "Say dog." I spoke in tongues. Then he said, "Say cat!" The other language poured out of me. At last, he got really inspired and got a piece of paper and a pencil and said, "Write what you are saying down!"

To my huge consternation, I filled the page with writing in another language. That somehow gave me the release I needed, and suddenly I could speak in English again. I was then able to explain to him what had happened. (I tell you, there is never a dull moment being married to me. People need to pray for Mike more than they do.)

The next morning, I had some of my girlfriends over for tea (which means iced tea for us) and snacks. We were sitting around the table, and I was showing them the paper and relating the story of the angel. One of my friends looked at the writing and thought she might know the interpretation. At that moment, our daughter came up to her and said something that was a question, and it started with "How come?"

One of the other ladies around the table grew very still and quiet for a moment and then quietly said, "I think I can interpret what you wrote on the paper." She said that when Mary had asked her "How come?" she knew she had the interpretation because when she had looked at the strange writing, she immediately heard these words in her mind: *In the past, I would have told you stay, but now I tell you come. I am going to open many doors for you.*

All I can say is that the Lord did open many supernatural doors for me from that day. I went from ministering to little children and leading worship in my local church to a worldwide ministry.

How did that happen? I must admit that God did not have a very willing subject with me. I had grown up as a preacher's kid, and I knew what they went through. God is nice, but pioneering can bring up the not nice in His children.

When one writes memoirs, it dredges up so much emotion. I must admit that I have stopped and cried a few times in writing this book of remembrance. It is more of a healing experience for me than I had any inkling it would be! Being vulnerable isn't always easy.

"Now Will You Go?"

Local ministry was one thing, but a traveling ministry meant a lot of things—being gone from home, figuring out how to be a super mom, and saving your kids from life's hurts, among many others. God was going to have to deal with me strongly to get a "Yes, I will go" out of this mom.

I was studying books on many subjects in those days, supplied to me by my friend Joyce Bogle. One of the books was about the life of Aimee Semple McPherson. If you do not know about her, she had a great evangelistic and healing ministry in the 1920s. Her life fascinated me. In one particular chapter, it told of her struggle to follow the call of God. It related how she resisted going and one day became sick unto death. They put her in a room where they put people to die, and then she heard the words, *Now will you go?* When she said yes, Aimee was instantly healed. I read that story and tucked it away in my heart. Little did I know God would use that story to have a big effect on me personally.

The Holy Spirit began to work in my heart to relinquish myself wholly to the call of God. Of course, as I wrote in my book *Women, Rise Up!*, I tried to negotiate with God and offered Mike to go in my place. You know, the old compromise, *Here I am, Lord. Send Mike!* (I know, I know—a really dumb thing to try, but at the time, it seemed feasible!)

This unrest in my heart would result in me walking the floors of our wooden house at 309 West Josephine Street, praying and struggling, while everyone else was asleep. At last, one dark night I cried out, "Lord, why me, a woman?!" Thoughts of the chapter I read in Sister Aimee's biography kind of wafted in my head. I mused, *Am I really willing to give my all for God?*

My Bible reading for that time was Matthew 16:24–25. Would I take up my cross and follow Him, no matter the cost? The answer to my question of "Why me?" was soon to come. Quietly, I heard the voice of the Lord say, *Because I need a woman, and I choose you.*

This passage, Joel 2:28–29, came to my mind:

> And it shall come to pass afterward,
> That I will pour out My Spirit on all flesh;
> Your sons and your daughters shall prophesy,
> Your old men shall dream dreams,
> Your young men shall see visions,
> And also on My menservants and on My maidservants
> I will pour out My Spirit in those days.

The Lord knew I believed the Scripture. What He was saying to me was biblically sound. Now I inwardly groaned, *Oh no! I am going to have to do this! God is asking for everything*. Everything meant that I needed to give the Lord my family and trust Him with them. That was hard—very, very hard.

As I mentioned, at that time I was a worship leader and teacher of children. I was going to find out that when one gives all to the Lord, He takes you up on it. I want to add at this point that surrendering to the Lord did not mean I was not still going to be a mother or abandon my children. It did mean that, at times, I was going to have to be away from them. When one is struggling with a calling, it is easy to find excuses to change the boundaries of the scope of the ministry and how you will fulfill it.

Since my degree was in music, that has always been a pull on me. One day I heard Christ For The Nations was hiring a new vocal teacher—right up my alley! I went for an interview and passed the first step. Later, at home, I sat down and played Rachmaninoff's "Mazurka," and when I finished, the Lord said to me, *Cindy, if you take that job, you will have to cancel a lot of meetings. The call to music is the call to your soul, but the call to preach is the call of your spirit. You can't take that job.*

I must admit that I cried as I gave my first love to the Lord—teaching music. Of course, it was the right thing to do. I recently watched a movie about a music teacher and was shocked that I found tears in my eyes. I loved teaching music so much!

Meanwhile, Back at Home

The thing about being a pioneer was that I really did not have anyone to ask the hard question about how to be a mom and a minister. Later on, when I met some women in ministry, none of them had children the same age as mine, or they were pastoring with their husbands. Another difficult thing was that we did not have any relatives who could help on a regular basis. My sister and her husband helped, and my mom and stepdad came at various times.

As a result, Mike and I learned some lessons the hard way. There were some people who did not treat our kids right. Some of this we only found out later. Another thing I learned was that I needed to check out the whole family, and not just my women friends who would be their primary caregivers. I have had to demand apologies from some men who were harsh with my kids.

Mike was still working full-time at the airlines and was not a guy who could cook, and he had never used the washing machine. Thank God for my girlfriends! They cooked meals for me, cleaned, and generally helped. This is not to say that I or we were gone extensively. But traveling even once or twice a month still had its challenges.

There are two kinds of memoirs. One glosses over the difficult times, and the other is a tell-all. I am trying to mentor in these pages, while not wanting to scare anyone away from the challenges of ministry. Someone asked me, "Was it hard?" Yes, at times it was very, very hard. I traveled quite a bit by myself and was often lonely in a hotel room. Mike and I tried for one of us to be there with the kids as much as possible.

How did we balance life with the kids? Juggling being a mommy and a minister came with unique challenges, but we put things in place as a family to stay close and enjoy each other. Every Wednesday night, we had a ritual. Mike and I took the kids to the pizza parlor before we went to church. (I was rarely gone on a Wednesday.) We also had a regular video night, when we went to Blockbuster and allowed each child to choose a video. In addition, we took the kids for walks in the park. We also got them a season pass to the pool around the corner, and they loved spending most of their summers in the water. Life was busy, yes, but it was also good and fun!

Things were easier when the kids got older. Was it worth it being spiritual pioneers while also raising a family? Yes, a thousand times yes! Would I have done some things differently? Absolutely! This is why I am being so honest. I think, in retrospect, I would have traveled less when the kids were small. The doors that flung open, like now, were so many.

God Was My Publicist

I remember telling a friend on the phone one day, "I feel like I am on a horse that is galloping faster than I want it to." For me, it felt like I went from no ministry invitations to hundreds—and that was before I even wrote my book *Possessing the Gates of the Enemy.* The invitations piled in.

I never asked to speak anywhere and never sent out my résumé to try to get a place to speak. God was my publicist. Unusual things happened to me, such as when I was visiting a church in Torrance, California, and met the head of the women's ministry before the meeting. After she greeted the people, she said, "We have a visitor today, and God has told me that she is supposed to speak today instead of me," and then she called me forward! What was I supposed to do? Well, I simply stood up and preached.

This was not the only time that happened to me. Once, my mother-in-law and I went to visit a women's meeting at a large church in Phoenix called the Valley Cathedral. The pastor over the women was Faye Darnell. I had met her earlier during a luncheon with her and Mom. The morning of the meeting, the Lord awakened me early and said, *I want you to fast today*. I didn't know why, but I did so. As the meeting got started, I felt the anointing pouring through me. I didn't know what to do with it all, so I released it into my mother-in-law. She fell out under the power of God.

Faye announced to the group that God told her I was to minister to the women that day. I started to pray for people and prophesy, and three hours later, almost everyone in the room of approximately one hundred women were out under the power. I felt as though I was walking through a thick presence as the glory of God filled the room. I remember one prophecy I gave that was quite unusual. It went, "You're dating someone in the Mafia, and you are afraid you will get killed. God says break up and I will protect you!" Wild word, huh? The woman said it was true!

After I went back to Texas, Faye called and asked me to speak for their annual women's retreat. Valley Cathedral was a megachurch, and she explained that they had always had well-known women ministers, but she felt I should be their speaker. I was stunned! I had never spoken more than one time anywhere, but now I would need to speak three times. Would I be able to do it? I was about to find out.

The retreat center was in Cornville, Arizona. It was lovely, and they had a special speaker's guest room. Before my time to speak, I must have worn a path in that room as I paced up and down in a bit of panic and fear. As I stood in the pulpit, I am sure my knees were shaking. I remember speaking on dealing with bitterness and bitter-root judgments. After the message, many were weeping and getting set free.

One of the most unusual manifestations I have seen to this day happened during that weekend. I was casting spirits out of a woman, and when I called out rejection, the demon manifested, pounded the floor, groaned, and said, "I am the last one," repeating it over and over. Dumb devil—now I knew for sure that what I had called out of the woman was right. The spirit of rejection soon was gone!

Coming back home and going to a parent-teacher association meeting was always a down-to-earth moment for me. The ladies in Weatherford would talk about canning peas and putting up preserves. When they asked me what I did over the weekend, what was I to say? "Oh, I cast out demons"? I would usually say simply, "Oh, I went out of town."

Pioneer Conferences on the Prophetic

One great joy for Mike and me has been our relationship with Chuck Pierce. We did one of the pioneer conferences on the prophetic, and that is how we met him. After that, his church in Denton, Texas, paid his salary to work with us three days a week. He also wrote for our Generals International newsletter, *GI News*. We would pray and ask God what areas of the world to focus on, and Chuck would write a prophetic article on that part of the world. To this day we are family.

When Mike was laid off from American Airlines, we had no income. The Lord told Mike that teaching was what we had in our hands to both be a blessing and further the ministry, so we started doing conferences. We had children to feed and a house payment to make.

For a pioneer conference on the prophetic, Chuck came to Weatherford with Robert Heidler and others from what was then Believers Fellowship (now Glory of Zion). He also got connected with Peter Wagner and Dutch Sheets at that time. Dutch was a speaker for our first prophetic conference.

We made manuals for spiritual warfare and other topics, and I wrote *Possessing the Gates of the Enemy*. From the time Mike left American Airlines, we never made less money than we did while he was working full-time. I also traveled and preached, but that brought in very little income at the time. To this day, I don't know how we made it, but God called us to work together, and we did.

10

Where Are the Generals?

In 1984, as I fasted and prayed for America, I asked the Lord, *How has Satan made so many inroads into the United States?*

The Lord answered me that Satan had a strategy, and His people did not. Then He expounded on the fact that there were many sins of the nation for which there needed to be repentance—sins such as slavery, the Japanese internment camps, etc.

Later on, John Dawson termed this kind of prayer "identificational repentance." The Lord then instructed me to gather the "generals" to repent for these sins. Generals are those who are prayer leaders in their churches and ministries. At that time, not many churches had intercessory prayer groups. The prayer groups were mainly composed of grandmothers who were faithful to pray in small groups. Very few ministries had organized prayer teams. Kenneth Copeland was a pioneer in this area. My friend Beth Alves was one of the first prayer leaders for his ministry.

I also felt from the Lord to start our meetings in Dallas, and then to expand our efforts into Tulsa, Oklahoma, and afterward into the Los Angeles area, and gather prayer leaders in each of those cities to intercede together. After that, we were to connect with Canada, Great Britain, and Australia.

I talked to Mike about the calling to gather the generals of intercession, and he agreed we should do it together. Now we just needed a place and meeting time. So I started making cold calls. I didn't know anyone—I simply started calling one ministry after another to find a place.

"Working the Word"

One thing Mike and I have learned is that when God calls you to do a thing, He will open the doors. You just have to fast and pray and then get up the courage to move out on the Word of God and any prophetic words. You have to "work the Word." This can be hard and, at times, downright discouraging! But don't give up!

During the 1980s, a pastor named Larry Lea started teaching on the Lord's Prayer. He had a church called Church on the Rock in Rockwall, Texas, and had become quite well-known for his teaching. I phoned his church and asked to speak to someone in charge of prayer. They connected me with their prayer leader, Dr. Bob Wilhite. I was delighted to share my vision with Bob, and he later became a good friend. He had been a mentor to Larry Lea and told me he would be glad to host a meeting of the generals at Church on the Rock.

I got on the phone again and started calling ministry after ministry in the Dallas–Fort Worth area. Most told me they did not have a prayer director, per se, but would send a representative. We finally set a date in the fall of 1985 for the gathering.

The night of the meeting, Mike and I drove an hour and a half to reach the host church. As we introduced ourselves, I realized I knew the beliefs of most of the ministries represented in that room. Some believed Christians could not be demonized; others believed a Christian could have anything they wanted—including demons! There were other nuanced beliefs as well.

I must admit, I was a bit nervous. There I sat, a thirty-four-year-old nobody with a vision. Clearly, I was the youngest in the room. Bob began with a statement that was inspired by God: "Even though we might have different beliefs, we can all agree that America needs a revival. Can we gather around the foot of the cross and come into unity around that understanding?"

It was as if those in the room gave a corporate sigh of relief. Bob made the way for me to share the vision in my heart. Other leaders shared the burdens on their hearts. God brought us to a sweet place of *koinonia*, a deep fellowship with one another. It was a great victory for intercessory prayer!

"Friendly" Phone Calls

Satan was lurking around the corner, however, to try to steal what had happened and stop me in my tracks. The next few days after the meeting, I started getting phone calls from "friends." One said to me, "My pastor said that if God was going to gather the generals, He would never use a woman your age." In other words, age was a disqualifier. Later, I thought of several Bible passages I could have quoted about God using young leaders—like God telling Jeremiah not to say he was just a youth. At the time, I was just too taken aback to have a good comeback.

The next day, I received another call from one of "Job's friends." This one said, "Well, my pastor says that even if God would use a young person to gather generals, He would never use a woman!" Ouch! That frankly stung. Too young—and the wrong gender.

At that point, I was undone. In girl talk, that means crying—ugly crying. You know, the kind that requires interpretation because your voice is so high and squeaky that it cannot be naturally understood.

Mike came home to find me in that condition. No doubt my mascara was running down my face, and my nose was red and running—not a pretty picture! Having been married twelve years, Mike had learned a thing or two about women. He went and got a handful of Kleenex and handed them to me. I wiped my nose, then my eyes, and worked to compose myself.

"Mike," I finally squeaked out, "I've made a horrible mistake." I went on to share that I thought God had said to gather the generals, but I was too young, and—the worst part—I was a woman.

My husband looked at me and said, "I'm going to pray and get a word from the Lord about this."

More Gatherings with the Generals

A couple of days later, Mike came back and said, "Cindy, God didn't call you because of your age or your gender. He called you because you love Him so much and will do anything He asks you to do." Then he reminded me of the story of young David and how he fought Goliath. "Honey, God did try to speak to others," he said, "but they simply would not pay the price. Now He has found you."

It's interesting how God will be faithful to console you, His child, after a trying—and perhaps even a testing—time. A third person called me, without any natural knowledge of the trial I had been through. She said she had been praying for me, and that

God had called me to do more gatherings with the generals—and not to let anyone tell me otherwise!

We began to have monthly meetings at different ministries in the Dallas area and would have special speakers share with us. I'll never forget the meeting with Mrs. Freda Lindsay, the president of Christ For The Nations Institute (CFNI). She was a Canadian whom God had called alongside her husband, Gordon, to start the school in Dallas. The night of our meeting with her, she prayed and asked God to connect Canada and the United States together. It was so powerful! We miss that mighty woman of God. (A few chapters ahead, I'll tell you more about the amazing prayer meetings we had at CFNI after we were called back to Texas. There is also a chapter ahead with more about Generals International.)

11

Enter the Wagners

Mike and I were invited to a prayer conference in Washington, DC, in 1989. Little did we know at the time, our whole life was going to be impacted during that event.

The night we arrived at the conference center seemed like any other. But I could hardly sleep because of the unusual excitement I felt. The only way I can explain is to compare it to how I felt as a child on Christmas Eve or the night before a family vacation—or all the above rolled into one. Now I understand the Holy Spirit was anticipating a glorious relationship that would begin the next day.

During the conference, historic speakers were taking the stage—people such as Joy Dawson, Dr. C. Peter Wagner, and others. During one session, I led a time of identificational repentance with a friend from England, Derek Brandt. This time, the United States was on the receiving end. He asked us, as US representatives, to forgive the iniquities of racism that had come from England at our founding.

After the meeting, Mike and I attended a board meeting for the newly created United States Prayer Center, headed up by Dr. Bob Wilhite. Peter Wagner introduced himself and his wife, Doris, to Mike and me, and we also met Len LeSourd, then vice president of Chosen Books. They offered us a ride to the meeting, as they were also on the board.

During the car ride through downtown Washington, Peter began asking me questions about the kind of praying he had witnessed the day before. At the time, he was researching prayer and had never seen anything like what had taken place. I answered his questions one by one. Then he asked if Mike and I would go to dinner with them after the meeting. We agreed—and a whole new world was about to open to us.

It's amazing how God arranges connections with people who carry synergy with our future destinies. Some relationships are like scaffolding—only present during a season of building. Others, like Esther and Mordecai, are foundational to our calling. What began that day would continue for more than thirty years. Peter passed away in 2016, but my relationship with Doris continues.

My Book Writing Begins

That day, Peter was used by God to answer an audacious prayer I had prayed. Several people had been encouraging me to write a book on prayer. Honestly, the thought intimidated me. So I had prayed, *Lord, if You want me to write a book, I need a mentor. Also, I don't want to have to find a publisher—bring one to me.*

Both parts of that prayer were answered the next afternoon. Peter looked at me with that commanding apostolic expression and said, "Cindy, I'm meeting with Chosen Books tomorrow afternoon at four. They want me to write a book on prayer. I just told them, 'You don't need my book—you need Cindy's.'"

Stunned, I recalled my bold prayer. There was no escaping now!

I had already met Len LeSourd, and now I was introduced to Jane Campbell, the acquisitions editor—just the person I needed to guide me through writing my first book. At the meeting, I agreed to write a few chapters and send in a book proposal letter. I had no idea what that meant. I had to learn. If there was hope for me, there's hope for you—if you're just beginning to write too!

Signing Up for Deep Waters

Shortly after we met Peter and Doris, he called and invited us to Pasadena, California, to teach his 120 Fellowship class at Lake Avenue Congregational Church. He had been teaching on the book of Acts and felt my gift of prophecy would help move the class from theory to practical application regarding the gifts of the Spirit.

He also asked if, while I was visiting, I would guest-lecture on spiritual warfare—specifically dealing with powers of darkness—for his class at Fuller Theological Seminary. I agreed, but as a thirty-eight-year-old, I had no idea just how deep the waters would be. I've said yes to many things in my life, only to nearly panic later when I realized what I had signed up for. Lecturing at Fuller was definitely one of those moments!

I spoke to both master of divinity and doctor of divinity students. The MDiv students were polite. The DMin students? Entirely different. Frankly, some of them were downright mean. As I taught on demonology, one student openly challenged me, saying, "There are no such things as demons today." But God had me covered—a pastor from Africa immediately responded, "She is exactly right. We deal with demon possession regularly in our churches." *Thank You, Lord, for having my back!*

Needless to say, I went back to the Wagners' house feeling battered. My soul did not—let me repeat—did *not* want to go back the next day for round two. But I did. I had made a promise. Be careful what you promise!

"Start Over!"

My stretching with the Wagners had only just begun. I had written three chapters of what would become my first book, *Possessing the Gates of the Enemy*, and brought them for Peter to review and give me feedback. What happened next was nothing short of discouraging. Peter invited me into his study—a fascinating room filled with souvenirs from his missionary days in Bolivia. I was already nervous. Then he looked at me, grinned, and held my manuscript over the trash can.

"Do you really want me to help you with this book?" he asked.

Everything in me wanted to run out of the room—until the phone rang. Peter had mentioned earlier that John Wimber had asked if Dick Mills could call and give him a word. Dick was known for giving prophetic words through Scripture and had memorized 770 passages in five translations.

Peter asked me, "Should I take the call?"

I said, "Yes—Dick is major league."

Dick prophesied to Peter, and then said, "Tell Cindy she is there by divine appointment, and anything Peter tells her to do, she must do."

Peter grinned and said, "Now, do you want me to help you or not?"

I nodded. He threw the manuscript in the trash and said, "Start over!" Then he pulled it back out, marked it up, and said, "Too much teaching, not enough stories. You only quote yourself. Do research. Include other authors."

So I tried again. I learned how to write a book proposal. To my surprise, Chosen Books sent me a contract. Wow! It was getting very real.

Writing Through Spiritual Warfare

Writing was hard. I faced all kinds of spiritual warfare. We were still using typewriters, carbon paper, and fax machines—no email, no Google. My kids were little, and I wrote early in the mornings and late at night. Both my typewriter and backup typewriter broke. Becky Wagner (now Systema) was helping me—her computer broke too. The fax machine failed. I finally said, "Satan, you're not stopping me!" and began writing by hand.

Eventually, I got it done, and Chosen Books published it. A friend read it and said, "I can't wait for your next book!"

I looked at her like she was from Mars. "Next book? Never!" But of course, more books followed.

Possessing the Gates of the Enemy was not an immediate bestseller due to the topic being so new. However, it was eventually translated into over thirty languages and helped launch prayer movements all around the world. Thank you, Peter, for pushing me toward my destiny—even when I wasn't sure I wanted to go.

That's what mentors do—they stretch us, provoke us to greatness, and at times frustrate us. There's no one like them, and I'm grateful to the Lord for sending me Peter Wagner.

Attending Lausanne II

One early highlight was the invitation that came through the Wagners for us to attend and participate in Lausanne II, which took place in 1989 in Manila, Philippines. Peter had the idea that the conference should feature a twenty-four-hour prayer watch throughout the entire event. I was asked to help lead it, along with Ben Jennings of Campus Crusade for Christ. Other leaders were spiritual giants such as Joy Dawson. As far as we knew, this was the first event of such massive size to be covered in day-and-night intercession.

I flew to the Philippines by myself, which was a bit of a stretch for me. I traveled on an airline pass, since Mike was still working for American Airlines at the time. We lived over an hour away from the airport, so I had to drive myself, and flying on a pass meant I could only board if there were empty seats after the standby passengers. It looked like I wasn't going to get on—they were about to close the flight. I prayed fervently, and at the last minute, I was able to board . . . in a middle seat between two very large men who kept falling asleep on my shoulders during the long flight. Needless to say, I was quite relieved when we landed. Thankfully, I found the event bus and made it to the hotel, where I met Peter and Doris.

I led so many prayer watches that I eventually got a little sick. The human body simply isn't meant to go without sleep for a full twenty-four-hour stretch! One of the most exciting moments was when, after much prayer, the Russian team finally arrived. In 1989, we had not yet been able to meet openly with our Russian brothers and sisters in Christ. There were tears all around.

During the conference, I also taught in the Spiritual Warfare track, which ended up being one of the most popular sessions.

The hall was packed every time. My topic was strategic-level spiritual warfare—how to deal with powers of darkness in the heavenly realms. Peter commented on the crowd by saying, "The people voted with their feet when it came to what they wanted to learn!"

One thing a good mentor does is connect you with leaders who can help advance your calling. During that trip, Peter introduced me to people who would later become significant parts of my life—Ed and Ruth Silvoso, Omar and Marfa Cabrera, and Jack Hayford.

Launching the Spiritual Warfare Network

As I mentioned, Peter was deeply involved in researching prayer in the 1990s. After Lausanne II, he invited me to a meeting at his office at the School of World Mission at Fuller Seminary. Gary Clark and John Robb believed a roundtable on spiritual warfare would bring significant advancement to the Kingdom—and they were right. The Spiritual Warfare Network (SWN) began at that roundtable and operated as an ad hoc committee of the Lausanne Movement.

I contributed by inviting many leaders from the charismatic side of the Body of Christ, including several women prayer leaders. I also assembled a team of intercessors to pray for the SWN meeting, including Dutch Sheets and Chuck Pierce. Roberta Byerly led the intercessors.

We met at Lake Avenue Congregational Church in Pasadena, where Peter held his 120 Fellowship class. The gathering was historic. Many people in that room would go on to write iconic books—John Dawson (*Taking Our Cities for God*), Ed Silvoso (*That None Should Perish*), Sister Gwen Shaw (*Redeeming the*

Land), Dick Eastman (*The Hour That Changes the World*), and George Otis Jr. (*The Last of the Giants*). I was right in the middle of writing *Possessing the Gates of the Enemy* at the time.

We continued meeting regularly for years. Among other things, we developed a shared glossary of terms and agreed to use consistent language in our teachings. We adopted George Otis Jr.'s term *spiritual mapping* and John Dawson's term *identificational repentance*. Dr. Charles Kraft—one of the conveners, along with Peter Wagner, Gary Clark, and myself—shared on what we later called ground-level spiritual warfare (casting out demons). We also discussed occult-level warfare and cosmic-level warfare—which became my area of focus as strategic-level warfare.

By our second meeting, Peter had begun discussions with Luis Bush and Thomas Wang about joining their new movement, AD2000 & Beyond, which aimed to reach the unreached people groups of the world by the year 2000. We voted to become part of the movement. The unity we developed during those gatherings was deep and lasting. We were in the trenches together, forming what would become a global prayer movement.

Picking Up the SWN Baton

These meetings continued from 1990 to 1996. One day, Peter called to say he was going to shut down the Spiritual Warfare Network. He felt his assignment was complete. I immediately pleaded, "Don't stop it, Peter—give it to me!" And he did.

We held a gathering of the SWN, and he publicly announced that I would be the new leader. One well-known ministry leader came up to me afterward and said, "Well, now you've got a big target on your back." Not very comforting.

When the baton is passed, it's up to the next leader to receive fresh strategy for the new season. We held our first official meeting under my leadership at Glen Eyrie Castle in Colorado Springs. It was a historic event, and many top leaders attended. (I'll write more about the Glen Eyrie meeting in the next chapter.)

It's remarkable how great gospel thrusts can emerge from key relationships. There's more to the story about the Wagners and Mike and me, and I'll pick up that thread up again in the next chapter, which talks about our years in Colorado Springs.

Cindy's parents, Eleanor and Albert Johnson, in 1947

1883 Exhorter's License to preach, from Cindy's mom's side. Along with her father, a legacy of preaching runs through both sides of her family.

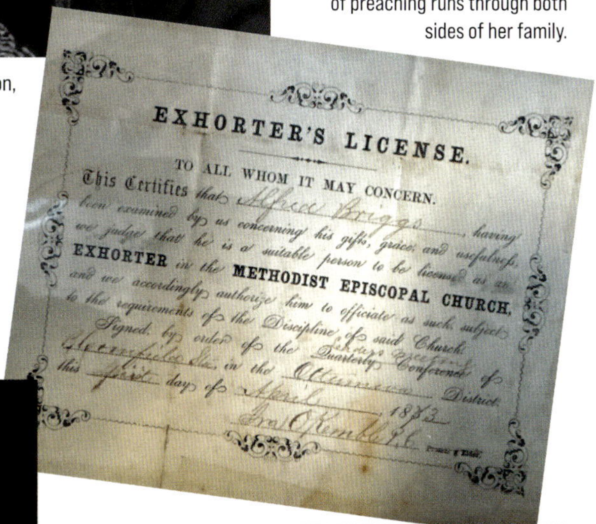

EXHORTER'S LICENSE.

TO ALL WHOM IT MAY CONCERN.

This Certifies that Alfred Briggs, having been examined by us concerning his gifts, grace and usefulness, we judge that he is a suitable person to be licensed as an EXHORTER in the METHODIST EPISCOPAL CHURCH, and we accordingly authorize him to officiate as such, subject to the requirements of the Discipline of said Church.

Signed, by order of the Quarterly Conference of Bloomfield Sta. in the Ottumwa District this first day of April, 1883

Geo. O. Kemble P.E.

Presiding Elder.

Cindy, 5 years old

Cindy's mom, Eleanor Johnson, brother-in-law and sister, Mark and Lucy Reithmiller, and Grandmother Lucile McJilton

Cindy and Mike's wedding, August 22, 1973. They had a small wedding at her professor's house.

Mike (35), Cindy (32), Mary (3), Daniel (6 months). Daniel is still in a cast.

Bob and Helen Jacobs (Mike's parents), Daniel (5), Mary (8), Mike (39)

Eleanor Johnson, Richard Johnson, Lucy Reithmiller (Cindy's mother, brother, and sister)

Mike, Cindy, and her father figure, Peter Wagner

Bishop Bill Hamon praying over
Mike and Cindy Jacobs

Cindy Jacobs at 36

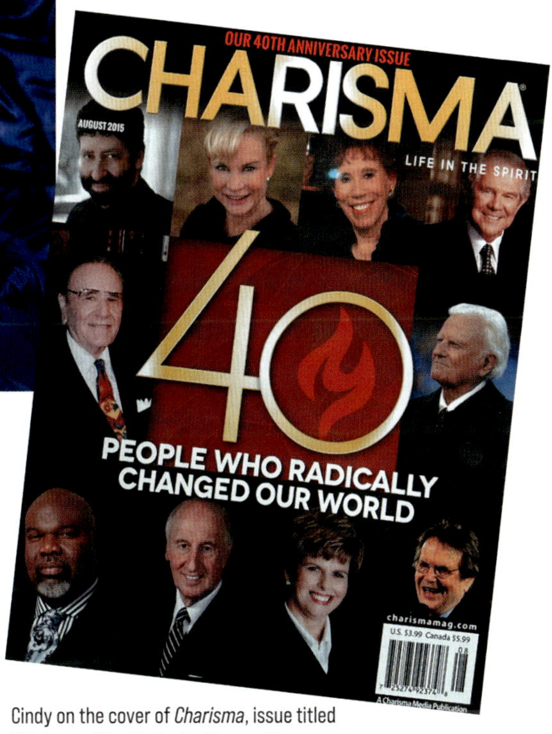

Cindy on the cover of *Charisma*, issue titled "40 People Who Radically Changed Our World"

Cindy Jacobs and Ed Silvoso speaking together in Argentina during the revival

Cindy Jacobs, Lou Engle, Bill and Beni Johnson, Ché and Sue Ahn ministering together

Mike and Cindy on their 50th wedding anniversary at their dream wedding

Daniel and Jenay Jacobs' wedding day

Cindy, Mike, and grandkids Lilli, Liam, and Wyatt Carlucci-Jacobs

Jenay, Dr. Chuck Pierce, Cindy, and Mike sharing God's wisdom on the set of Cindy's new show *Double Portion*

Daniel, Cindy holding her only granddaughter, Lilli, Mary and her boys, Caden, Malachi, Zion

Onstage at GI event, Wyatt, Daniel, Liam, Mike, Cindy, Lilli, and Jenay

Larry Sparks, Tommy and Miriam Evans, Ché Ahn, Jenay, Mercedes Sparks, Dutch Sheets, Cindy and Mike after ministering together

Cindy and Bishop Joseph Garlington ministering together at our yearly Global Prophetic Summit gathering

Cindy, Mike, and Werner Nachtigal at the Ninety-Five Theses door of the Wittenberg, Germany, cathedral, where Martin Luther started the Protestant Reformation

Ed and Ruth Silvoso, Cindy and Mike Jacobs on the set of Cindy's show

Cindy at the pyramids in Egypt filming for her new GITV app

Cindy and Jenay filming in Italy for her prophetic show *When Heaven Hears*

Cindy ministering in Malaysia, fulfilling her call to the nations—bringing hope from the Lord around the world each year

Cindy ministering in Brazil

Cindy at the Great Wall of China

Liam, Wyatt, Jenay, Cindy, Jeff (Jenay's brother), Mike, Janina (Jenay's Mom), Lilli, Daniel

Cindy and Mike at the Gala Awards Dinner for Israel

Cindy recording in our new studio, nurturing and equipping others from the *General's Desk*

12

The Colorado Springs Era

Mike and I were happy living in Weatherford, and had never really considered moving anywhere else, when I began to feel a call to move to Colorado Springs. At that time, our good friend Dick Eastman had moved the ministry he headed, Every Home for Christ, to the Springs. He was going to build a new ministry headquarters and invited us to be part of it and to move our ministry into the building, called the Jericho Center.

At first, I was the lone voice in the family regarding the move. I remember having dinner one night when the kids began chiming in on the subject: "Dad, Mom says we should move to Colorado Springs! We don't want to move! All our friends are here." To which Mike replied that he hadn't heard anything about moving.

Eventually, we got on the same page. This brings up the theme of teamwork in marriage—especially when your wife is a prophet. Mike is kind of like my brakes—in a good way. We have found I usually hear things first, but God uses Mike to bring the timing.

There have been a few times when it was the other way around, but that's rare.

Of course, we thought the Weatherford house would sell quickly. We were wrong. It took two years before we were able to make the move. When we finally got an offer on our old wooden house, the buyers were using a government loan with very stringent requirements. For one, we had an old shed in the back that had to be torn down. Also, the house had a pier and beam foundation that needed a lot of reinforcement. Mike crawled under the house with his buddies, and they did the work themselves. Thank God for friends! We finally closed on the house in 1993.

"This Is It!"

In the meantime, Mike went looking for a home in Colorado. I was traveling extensively, so he took the lead. I'm not the easiest person to shop for, and he kept sending me pictures—but the homes would sell within hours. At last, we pulled up to a house that a friend of a friend had listed for sale by owner. I stood in the foyer of it, only the second house we had visited together, and said to Mike, "This is it!"

He asked, "Don't you want to see the rest?" Of course I did, but I knew the moment I stepped in that we had found our home.

We didn't have enough furniture to fill it. I had asked God for four bedrooms and two and a half baths. He gave us six bedrooms and three and a half baths. We filled that house with young people living with us, and we hosted many meetings. At first, we even had the ministry in the basement. Becky Wagner (now Systema) worked in that basement. Eventually, I had enough of having the ministry in our home, and we began looking for offices. The

Jericho Center wasn't built until much later, and by that time we had outgrown the space they could offer us.

Our first office was off List Drive, and it was roomy at the time. But as we grew, we began looking for more space and eventually found a six-thousand-square-foot building on Garden of the Gods Road. We named it the Josiah Center, after the reformer king. It had plenty of room, and we hosted many meetings there and shared the space with other ministries.

During that era, Colorado Springs became a magnet for ministries. It was beautiful and fostered synergy. Peter and Doris Wagner moved there, as did Chuck Pierce and his family. Dutch Sheets had already arrived and later became pastor of Springs Harvest Fellowship, later known as Freedom Church.

Looking back, it was an exciting time—but also painful. We had no idea the path we were stepping into, launching massive thrusts into the global spiritual warfare and prophetic movements.

The World Prayer Center

Mike and I had lived in the Springs for about three years when Peter and Doris Wagner began talking about partnering with some others to build what became the World Prayer Center (WPC). Several of us felt it should be built on neutral ground, not an existing church property. But it was eventually built on the New Life Church campus.

The WPC building was stunning, though ultimately it wasn't used as originally envisioned. Peter and Doris raised over a million dollars for the project and were told Peter's offices could stay there for the rest of his life.

The Wagners did conduct their ministry from that location for a while, and Chuck Pierce also became vice president of Global Spheres during this time. Eventually, however, Peter and Doris relocated their offices.

In the late 1990s and early 2000s, Peter and Doris began hosting groundbreaking conferences on spiritual warfare and the prophetic. To this day, I hear of major ministries that were birthed from those gatherings.

A True but Troubling Prophetic Word

For some time, I had felt led to gather prophets from different streams to get to know each other and receive a corporate word from the Lord. In 1999, I asked Peter if I could use his name on the invitation as cohost for a prophets' roundtable. To our knowledge, it was the first of its kind. I also invited Bishop Bill Hamon, whom we regard as the father of the modern-day prophetic movement. He, too, had been thinking of doing something similar.

One reason we met was due to global panic over Y2K. People were stockpiling food, and many Christians were meeting about it. According to experts, computers couldn't compute the year 2000 and would shut down.

We met at New Life Church in Colorado Springs—about twenty of us. When we asked about the potential global crisis, the prophets sensed that something cataclysmic was coming, but not Y2K. Three leaders had dreams about an attack on US soil. One dream involved an ocean liner headed for the East Coast that was going to crash, with people jumping off. We asked the Lord if the attack could be stopped, and He said through prophet Jim Laffoon that it couldn't, but it could be lessened.

It was a true prophetic word. On September 11, 2001, at 7:46 a.m., tragedy struck. Al-Qaeda flew planes into New York City's Twin Towers in a suicide mission. Some intercessors praying near Trinity Church in New York City called me the night before to say they had seen two demonic principalities wrapping chains around the towers. "Cindy, something terrible is coming, and we can't stop it," they said.

There were reports of people who didn't go to work that day as a result. But many died. After hearing the prophetic word, we had fallen on our faces in intercession. I began weeping in travail and heard someone sobbing next to me—James Goll, a seer and prolific author. We became friends after that.

Part of a prophet's job is to watch over his or her nation. Joel 2:1 says, "Blow the trumpet in Zion. . . . Sound an alarm!" Over forty years of ministry, I've learned when to sound the alarm publicly and when to keep it quiet. Some things God tells us to share, some He tells us to keep. When God wants the alarm sounded, He will open the right door. Anytime I receive a strong word or alarm, I check it with the Apostolic Council of Prophetic Elders (ACPE), which was formed in 1999.

Ongoing Prophetic Roundtables

There are times when God calls a group to meet and it is a one-time thing. I have usually found it works best if I don't announce my intentions about the ongoing purposes of a particular meeting. Then, if during the meeting the Holy Spirit seems to prompt us to meet again, we can talk about it. Of course, there are variables to this, such as when God gives you clear guidance ahead of time to start a church or network.

After our first prophets' roundtable, we did agree to meet a second time. During the first meeting, however, we all felt we should ask Peter Wagner to be our apostle. It is scriptural to do so. Ephesians gives us the connection regarding apostles and prophets: "Having been built on the foundation of the apostles and prophets, Jesus Christ Himself being the chief cornerstone" (Ephesians 2:20).

In the late 1990s, we were just grappling in our connected networks as to what the relationships between apostles and prophets should look like. Peter did an excellent job navigating this, and for many years he would start the prophetic roundtables with an apostolic devotional of things God had put on his heart for the Body of Christ. After that, he often exclaimed, "It was like herding cats from there!"

If you have ever been in a room with a whole group of prophets, you will know what that means—it is a truism! Peter gave the leadership of the ACPE over to me in 2015, and since that time, I can personally say this is a fact! While prophets are very obedient corporately, they tend to be in a corner prophesying, and we have to round them up to convene again after a meal.

The 10/40 Window Prayer Initiative

One of the most exciting efforts actually started in Pasadena, California, while Peter was at Fuller Theological Seminary. The Spiritual Warfare Network, which I wrote about earlier, developed from a roundtable for discussion about a worldwide prayer ministry under the AD2000 & Beyond movement, led by Thomas Wang and Luis Bush. This culminated with the 10/40 Window prayer initiative.

The 10/40 Window is named for a global region bounded by the 10° and 40° north latitudes that is home to the least-reached people groups in the world. Prayer teams went on-site to pray, and it was glorious. In addition, every nation in the world was prayed for. The culminating event was a four-hour worship service that took place in the same amphitheater in Ephesus where the riotous crowd in Acts 19 had worshiped the goddess Diana for two hours (see vv. 23–41).

It is interesting to see how that worship service came about. One day, I went to visit Peter and Doris in their beautiful home on six acres in the Black Forest area of the Springs. He showed me pictures from their visit to Ephesus and said, "God told me that someday a group would worship Him for four hours in the same place they worshiped Diana for two hours."

I looked at him and said, "Peter, let's do that!"

He replied, "Do you want to?"

"Yes!" I exclaimed. And we did! I also said, "Why don't we ask Pastor Kim, the great Methodist pastor from South Korea, to bring his choir to end with the 'Hallelujah Chorus'?"

Peter asked him, he said yes, and the rest is history. I will never forget that day for as long as I live. What a great example of a prophet working with an apostle!

Letting God Take Over

I believe Colorado Springs was a place of refining for me. There was a person there who was accusing me of being in serious error. One of the accusations against me was that I was a false prophet. I wanted so much to be vindicated!

One day, I was so upset about the whole situation that I decided to ask for a public statement from known leaders as to whether they thought I was a true prophet. That was my flesh wanting vindication, however, and was not from God. The next morning, my Bible reading included Matthew 5:44–46: “It is easy to love those who love you, but I say, love your enemies and do good to them who despitefully use you” (my paraphrase). For a long time after that, I began reaffirming my forgiveness for my accuser every time I took Communion.

I knew I had to drop the whole thing and let God take over. Later, the Lord called me to really intercede for and bless this pastor. I didn’t want to. When I protested about having to pray for the one who had so maligned me, the Lord said, *Then don’t ever preach the message of the cross again, because you don’t understand how I would die for those who were crucifying Me.*

Ouch! I prayed until I could truly bless the man. This was a wilderness experience for me.

A Gathering of Historymakers

As I mentioned, I asked Peter to give me the Spiritual Warfare Network gatherings. In 1996, we did a by-invitation gathering at the lovely Glen Eyrie Castle, built by the founder of Colorado Springs, General William Jackson Palmer. By then the castle was the ministry headquarters of The Navigators. The grounds are simply stunning, with mountain sheep wandering around on the premises and a beautiful canyon.

Now that I look back, we were honored to have gathered some of the most important historymakers of our time. Among them were the pioneers of the inner healing movement, John and Paula Sandford. Also, Dutch Sheets of Give Him 15, Sister Gwen Shaw, founder of the End-Time Handmaidens, and Chuck Pierce of Glory of Zion. During that time, our friend Paul Tan came to me and prophesied that we would start a fifty-state prayer movement. We took that to heart and began to find coordinators, or prayer generals, as our ministry was originally called Generals of Intercession. (Our board voted to change it to Generals International around 2003, to broaden the vision to include the nations and the mentoring of prophets around the world.)

How do you find a prayer leader for every state? To keep things in perspective, in those days there weren't the networks of intercessors that we see today. It was pioneering. We hired Jill Griffin (now Mitchell) to help us identify leaders in all fifty states. We found them by asking friends and finding out whom they knew. Somehow, one person knew another, until we had all fifty. I must admit, it is still challenging today to keep a full fifty-state contingency. People get tired, they age out, and they have various life challenges.

We have also changed the name of the movement twice since then. It was initially the Spiritual Warfare Network, and then the Strategic Prayer Network. Then finally it became the Reformation Prayer Network, as it is called today, which is divided into fourteen regions of the United States.

Prayer Initiatives Through the Years

Through the years, we have done numerous prayer initiatives—most of which we never let anyone know we were doing. One such initiative was praying on-site at every abortion clinic in America. This prayer, along with the great work of Lou Engle and The Call events, and along with Matt Lockett's Justice House of Prayer (whose group stood in front of the Supreme Court every week for eighteen years), saw the federal law that had legalized abortion, *Roe v. Wade*, be overturned.

We have done two major initiatives concerning the US economy. One was in 2008. While in a worship service one Sunday morning in our church in Texas, God spoke to me and said, *There will be no more business as usual. Mobilize prayer on-site at Wall Street on October 29 this year.*

And we did. Little did I know there would be an economic crash on September 11, 2008, that would shake the economic systems of the world. There was literally no business as usual.

After the Lord gave me that ominous warning, I went to work mobilizing. I realized any crash in the US stock market would affect the whole globe, so our work had to be on a global level. How do you help heal the economy of the world? To begin with, you ask for advice from economists. We asked Jerry Tuma, who later wrote the book *From Boom to Bust and Beyond*, to advise us how to pray.

We went to Wall Street on October 29, 2008. Why that date? In US history, it is called Black Tuesday, as it was the day of the stock market crash in 1929 that caused the Great Depression. Every American never wants another Great Depression, as we have all seen pictures of the soup lines and the long, long job lines where people waited to get work.

By the time we got to Wall Street in 2008, the markets had crashed and a worldwide meltdown spiraled seemingly out of control. However, we had a strategy because we'd had warning. The warning hadn't included the actual date an event was going to happen, but we had prepared to pray.

Here is what we did: We went live on GOD TV and hosted a conference in Brooklyn to teach on prayer and healing economic structures. Then their cameraman followed us on-site as we prayed outside the stock exchange. In fact, we actually got onto the trading floor and found that people were hungry for prayer. They simply did not know what to do! It was a powerful time of intercession as well.

Afterward, we went up the street to the Charging Bull statue, the symbol of the stock market. We found out it was originally a noncommissioned piece that was "left" at Wall Street. This kind of art is called guerilla art. The city eventually moved it up the street. People come from all over the world to rub its nose for luck. We interceded about the spirit behind the art and realized it was Baal. Strangely, the news media followed us there too and reported we went there to worship the bull! A group of Christians picked that up and also believed we were worshiping the bull. Oh well, it happens! One must have the hide of a rhinoceros and the heart of a dove in ministry—especially the more visible you get in the media.

13

Texas Calling Again!

All my life, there seems to have been a rhythm to my returning to Texas. It was never something planned—except that God has given us inheritance here.

Mike and I thought we would live in Colorado Springs for the rest of our lives. We loved it! It is such a beautiful city, and we bought eight wooded acres on which to build our forever home. God had supernaturally helped us pay off the property, and we walked the land and dreamed. I took my first grandchild there and told him about it. We planned to put down roots in a part of the city called the Black Forest. It was where Peter and Doris had their home, and we were excited. But God has a way of showing us that our ways are not His ways.

One day, I received a prophecy from our good friend Sam Brassfield about where home would be for us. He sent it in August, and I must confess that I didn't show it to Mike until December. I was still "weighing it" in my mind. Obviously, that was not very spiritual of me. I liked our beautiful wooded property. My dreams and heart were set there.

In November, Mike and I went to TheCall Dallas, put on by Lou Engle. It was held in the Cotton Bowl Stadium. While there, we received a prophecy that God was going to give us the keys to two airplanes at Love Field, an airport in Dallas. The Lord knows how to get Mike's attention, as he is a private pilot and loves airplanes.

I had already been feeling as though Dallas was home instead of Colorado Springs, but I was pretty successful at ignoring it. When we received that prophecy, I knew I had to show Mike the earlier prophecy from Sam. The gist of it was that we were supposed to move back to the Dallas area, but this time, we were to move closer to Dallas than where we had lived previously, which was nearer to the twin city of Fort Worth. Our good friend Chuck Pierce had already moved back to Texas from Colorado Springs. When we showed him the prophecy, he immediately prophesied we were to move back by June 21, 2004.

When Chuck gave us that word, it was the end of January. We had to pack up the ministry, sell our home, and relocate our staff. This was a tall order!

All this to say that Mike worked hard at meeting that goal, and he rolled out the day before the deadline to move all our belongings to Texas. The house sold without ever being on the market. We asked for a sign from the Lord—that if we were to sell our property, we would put an ad in the newspaper, and it would sell quickly. It sold immediately for $10,000 over our asking price to someone who called us that day. God was in the move.

Where to move in Dallas was a big question. We decided we would look near the airport, but nothing seemed to open. God once again supernaturally moved and had us meet the mayor of Red Oak, which is in south Dallas, where we eventually had our offices. We knew, even though it meant a forty-five-minute drive, that was where we should be.

Miss Miracle and the Settlers' Stories

When we went to pray to see if God wanted us to buy a house near Red Oak, we stopped in a town called Ovilla. It is very tiny and has practically no downtown. We went into a little country store, and I saw a book on the history of Ovilla. It was written by a lady named Miss Miracle. After inquiring if someone knew her, the owner said, "Yes, I do!" A few minutes later, we were sitting on the front porch with Miss Miracle. Our friends James Goll and Sam and Linda Caster were with us. I asked Miss Miracle, "How did you get your name?"

She said, "Honey, I come from a long line of preachers." She proceeded to regale us with stories of the town. It was founded in 1844 by settlers who came from the Cane Ridge Revival in Kentucky. They felt they were to bring God to this area. At the time, Dallas was just a small outpost.

Miss Miracle told us the story of one of the settlers being awakened in the night with the deep conviction that she wasn't saved. It was around three a.m. She insisted on going from settler to settler to tell them they needed Jesus. This resulted in a great move of God among the pioneers. Perhaps they were the children of those who were in the Kentucky revival—I don't have those details. However, she became the first woman preacher that we know of in the whole Dallas area. The revival was called the Shiloh Revival. The settlers would call for preachers from the Cane Ridge Revival to preach in Brush Arbor meetings right around the corner from where we were sitting. There's a street named Shiloh, and a creek named Shiloh where they baptized the converts. We had hit a well of revival, and we hadn't known it! Now we did.

Fast-forward twenty-one years, and we own a beautiful eight-acre property in Ovilla, right down the way from the move of God, and we call it Shiloh. God is good! It's worth the drive to the airport to help redig the wells of the move of God in Texas.

Mike had gone house hunting while I was preaching. He showed me pictures on the web, and I said of our place, "Buy it," sight unseen. Prophets are strange creatures! When Mike had gone to look for houses in Colorado and I would look at them, I would just walk in the entryway and say, "Nope, this isn't it!" I believe Mike is going to get a gold star in his crown in heaven just for being married to me!

Redigging the Wells of Revival

One part of the prophecy Sam Brassfield had given us even before TheCall was that we were to move back to the Dallas area to "redig" the wells of revival. Genesis 26:18 references this: "And Isaac dug again the wells of water which they had dug in the days of Abraham his father, for the Philistines had stopped them up after the death of Abraham. He called them by the names which his father had called them."

The principle is this: There are moves of God that have gone on before us, and through time, the enemy brings sin to stop them up. Another generation comes along, and God calls them to build on what went on before and open up the wells of the Holy Spirit to flow again.

Dallas has seen many revivals. It has been prophesied by Ruth Ward Heflin in her book *Glory* that it would host the last and great revival. We know the whole Dallas–Fort Worth area will be an inheritor of that prophecy. Maria Woodworth-Etter had powerful meetings here in south Dallas, as well as Kathryn Kuhlman, Oral Roberts, Aimee Semple McPherson, F. F. Bosworth, and others. Gordon Lindsay founded the Voice of Healing movement in 1948 from here with a roundtable of healing evangelists. He started Christ For The Nations Institute out of that movement.

How does one respond to such a word—"redig the wells of revival"? I knew the word had to be acted upon and that CFNI was the place to do it. This school is a significant well that brought many evangelists together, such as Kenneth Hagin, Oral Roberts, Morris Cerullo, A. A. Allen, and others. When I asked God for the strategy, He put it on my heart to do forty days of prayer and fasting for miracles.

"Need Miracles? Got Miracles."

CFNI let us use their library chapel for our 40 Days of Prayer, which took place in 2005. (Years later, I gave my collection of around five hundred books to Christ For The Nations for that same library.) I wrote a prayer guide for the forty days, with a special focus on a specific healing Scripture passage for each day. We went all out and put ads on the screens of eighty-eight movie theaters, as well as in the *Dallas Morning News*, and put up a large billboard right by the school. Our team wore T-shirts that read "Will starve for miracles!" The ads said "Need miracles? Got miracles."

In the library chapel, we set up prayer stations with large swaths of paper hanging from the ceiling, where we would post pictures of people who needed prayer. One was for deliverance from demonic powers, another for salvation and healing, and another with large pictures of the revivalists who had preached in Dallas. Each session, the intercessors would move from station to station, praying over the pictures. There were finally so many posted after forty days that they were covering portions of the wall and floor.

After a while, people would post a picture, and the prayers would be answered almost immediately. We also had a twenty-four-hour chat room, where people could listen live and post their prayers. We had Chinese-speaking watches, Spanish-speaking watches, African watches, youth watches, children's watches, and many others.

Dramatic healings took place among those who came and prayed. One young boy with a neurological disorder was completely healed, went home, started learning again on his own, and became verbal. When we asked his parents what the initial signs of his healing were, they replied, "He stayed the whole time when multiple drums were being used in the prayer room. He would never have been able to stand the noise before he got healed!"

The last ten nights, the miracles flowed. We held meetings in the large auditorium of the school. One of the CFNI founders, Freda Lindsay, said that never in the history of the school had there been that many people who came for a meeting. The balconies were packed, and we had an overflow room across the street, where the same miracles were happening there as in the big auditorium. Mike went across the street the last night because somehow the feed had gotten turned off. The police said they had turned away at least one thousand people. God was on the move, and our prayers fueled the fire. Evangelists came, such as Steve Hill, who was instrumental in the Brownsville Revival, as well as the pastor from that church, John Kilpatrick.

The evening Pastor John preached, we asked him to share revival stories. As shared, the platform where we were sitting started to shake. This went on for about fifteen minutes. At first I thought, *There must be an air-conditioning unit under it.* I asked one of the leaders who had been there when it was installed, and he said, "No, there is nothing under the platform." It was the power of God—an Acts 4:31 moment: "And when they had prayed, the place where they were assembled together was shaken; and they were all filled with the Holy Spirit, and they spoke the word of God with boldness."

I went up to Pastor John and said, "John, the platform is shaking!" At that, he fell under the power of God, and it was like a Holy Spirit bomb had hit the place. People were falling out under the power all over the room. One leader who was sitting on the platform was thrown completely out of her shoes! I have never seen anything like it before or since.

The miracles were so many that on the last night, people were lined up in both aisles from the front of the auditorium to the back. A person with a broken back was healed; another person had flat feet and received new arches. Every kind of miracle you can imagine took place during those ten nights. After that, churches started exploding in growth all over the Dallas–Fort Worth metroplex. The power of God was evident. Over one hundred churches, from sixty nations, participated.

One testimony was overheard in a coffee shop near the school. It was reported to us that a policeman said he didn't know what was happening, but there was no crime in the troubled area where he was assigned duty. The atmosphere had changed! The worship had opened the heavens.

Two worship leaders who particularly sacrificed were Gabriel Allred and Rick Pino. Rick had graduated from the school and slept in his van during sets and showered in his buddy's room, and out of that 40 Days of Prayer came worship songs he later recorded. Gabriel became the worship leader at CFNI and served for six years. God rewards faithfulness. To this day, people tell us how their lives were totally changed during the 40 Days of Prayer.

14

Where Are the Deborahs?

Another part of Sam Brassfield's prophecy was that we would establish women leaders and minister to women, and that a movement would come out of Dallas for women. I had already launched the beginnings of this in 2001. Our first meeting was in Phoenix, which in many ways was a full-circle moment for me, as that was where Daddy had pioneered a work.

Our good friends Hal and Cheryl Sacks live in Phoenix, and they helped us find a facility and a worship team and filled in the gaps for other parts of that first meeting. It was called the International Coalition of Women Leaders.

It's interesting to note that another similar meeting had already been established by Iverna Tompkins, a great woman leader and pioneer who is now with the Lord. At the time we started, I contacted her to ask if she was going to do any more meetings, and she said no—so I felt the green light to go ahead.

Mike and I have always believed that ministry should be in covenant with others. We have rescheduled our meetings when we found that Peter Wagner or others were planning a meeting at the same time. I know this isn't always possible. Yet when you can, it is important to ascertain who your covenantal circle should be, and coordinate and collaborate with them. I remember one time Dutch Sheets moved his meeting for us because we had already put down deposits on a facility and he had not yet done so.

God made serious connections among the women leaders who came to that meeting. It was really the who's who of that generation. I had purposed in my heart I was not even going to tell the speakers ahead of time that they were going to speak, but simply trust God to give them a message when called upon. It worked—and it was powerful!

I had invited one woman to share about ministering to Muslim women. She and her husband were medical missionaries to Afghanistan. She had brought a burqa with her and held it up, saying, "Who will see that these women are free from this bondage?" Women rushed forward to receive a piece of that burqa and wept for the women who were captured in Islam. That night, I made a vow to God to take one million Muslims to heaven with me. I'm not sure where I am on that journey, but we helped Christian television in Arabic go out all across the Middle East. My dear friend Yvette Isaacs was my voice for many years. Mike and I are still working across North Africa and the Middle East to this day and have been to several nations in that region, as well as to Indonesia and Malaysia. I have found many Muslim women are lovely and kind. While I respect their right to wear the burqa, I don't think it should be forced on them by law.

One night as we were having a fire tunnel (this is where people line up across from each other, and those who pass through are prayed for by all), the air-conditioning broke in the ballroom. Remember, this was Phoenix in July, and it was steaming hot. Mike, being the resourceful guy he is, borrowed box fans from the hotel, and the men held them up to circulate the air. He always says that real women don't sweat—they mist!

The Deborahs Company

I can truthfully say that women were launched to minister across the world that weekend. We also had meetings for the young women. The dialogue was rich and sweet. I find that a leader taking time to sit with the next generation in dialogue is very important. My time in doing so has been part of producing leaders who are changing the world. For a number of years we had a Young Deborahs movement. We also had a Little Debbies project, with a course on etiquette for young women whose families had no idea what good manners were—how to host dinners and parties and have good conversation. There is definitely an art to having a good conversation, and it can be learned.

After that time, we changed the name to The Deborahs Company—or Deb Co, as we affectionately called it. We launched our first international chapter with high tea at the House of Lords in London. It was all very posh.

By then, our theme was "We pray, we change nations, and we buy shoes." We got some pushback about the buying shoes part. However, we did buy literally hundreds of pairs of shoes for people in various nations. Australia had great meetings with Teresa Tay, as well as Hong Kong with Yuk Lynn Woo, and preliminary meetings in Indonesia, Thailand, and Israel. My sister hosted a number of meetings in Minnesota, and Arizona grew strongly under the leadership of Stephanie Fullerton and Cindy

Carnahan. Cheryl Sacks also helped. The reach in other states like New York grew as well.

Philanthropy was and is a big part of the movement. We raised money to build a sewing machine factory for women in Pakistan. This was specifically for women who had been "honor raped" by Muslim men. They were considered untouchable and had trouble finding work. Another of our projects was funding a medical clinic in Garbage City in Egypt. The people in that city make their living by sorting through garbage and recycling it.

Deb Co in Jericho

One of our most satisfying projects was supplying baby formula and diapers to al-Qaeda women and children and refugees in Jericho. We had the infant supplies in a metal shed. The women came pouring in to get the baby formula and diapers and were getting a bit rowdy. When we ran out of relief products, we peered out and realized we might be in huge trouble. I told the ladies who were helping, "Let's lock arms, and when I tell you, make a loud noise and run for the bus." It worked! The restless women were so startled by our behavior that we were able to make it safely on board and quickly leave.

While we were in Jericho, some women asked to be baptized in the water source that Elisha had healed when it was bitter and became sweet. So we held a spontaneous baptism. The power of God hit that water, and we were transformed! The city still uses the water Elisha healed today. We were pretty soaked once we got on the bus—but nobody cared!

We also went up the Mount of Transfiguration, and Jill Austin and I started praying and crying out to God for the city. A picture was taken that day of a bolt of light that came out of the sky and touched our heads. Supernatural adventures with the Debs!

Raising Up Women Leaders

I have been a member of various organizations of leaders, and it seems to me that in past times, it was much harder to get women leaders to keep meeting together than it was to get men to meet. Various women had started meetings, and some even used the model we started, but the meetings never seemed to go anywhere. It can be a challenge as women, wives, and mothers to meet together. We have been able to meet for many years with the Deborahs, however, and we have started works on a worldwide scale. Some of the works progressed and some did not, but they all made an impact, and women leaders were raised up.

Our most successful meetings, I feel, were the ones started in the United Kingdom by my dear friend Julie Anderson. Julie and I met supernaturally when I lived in Weatherford. I received a picture of her and her husband through the mail when they were speaking at Calvary Cathedral in Fort Worth, and the Lord told me they would help bring revival to the United Kingdom. Shortly afterward I went to California, and my friend had the Andersons' wedding picture up in her house. When I saw it, she told me who they were, and then she connected me with them.

One night around midnight, I was home in Weatherford when my phone rang. It was Julie. I really didn't know much about her past, but I started prophesying that God would bring a new sound out of England that would have a greater impact than even the Beatles.

At that, Julie started sobbing out loud. At the time, I had no idea she had been the secretary for the Beatles' manager, knew the Rolling Stones, and had been in the office when the Beatles looked at a map and said, "We are more popular than God." Julie picked up the baton for the Deborahs and did many wonderful events in Westminster Chapel. Our favorite was called The War Horses. We were indeed the war horses for our generation.

Young Debs Grow into Leadership

What could women leaders do if they worked together? We dreamed. We met and shared our lives. We laughed a lot. We also dreamed of being a force for good. Having been one of the pioneers for women in leadership, I personally think it's deeply satisfying to see the young women who started out with us in their youth—whom we called our Young Debs—grow to be substantial leaders on their own.

These are some of the Young Debs now in leadership: Pastor Michele Jackson has taken over Hope Christian Church in Maryland since her father, Bishop Harry Jackson, passed away. Laura Allred has been given the Million Women movement after a successful October 12, 2024, event in Washington, DC, where 250,000 were in attendance and 10 million around the world joined us in praying for the US elections as we repented and prayed. Our own daughter-in-law, Jenay, has written her first book and now produces our made-for-Hollywood show *When Heaven Hears*.

Other women have also made great advances and now have their own ministries. Dehavilland Ford founded the 818 the Sign movement and now pastors Mercy Culture East in Fort Worth with her husband, Will. Jolene Hamill and her journalist and coauthor husband, Jon, founded Lamplighter Ministries and have made a major impact in praying for America.

Making a Difference Together

One of the most fruitful events we hosted for young women leaders was a by-invitation-only roundtable. During that meeting time, we discussed topics such as the challenges they faced as women leaders, what they felt was a generation affected by entitlement, and more. Then we would end up at my house eating pizza, with lots of laughs and sweet fellowship.

A really fun and strategic outgrowth of what later became the Deborahs United movement was one called Red Shoe Votes, where we held roundtables rallying women to vote for pro-life candidates. We provided voter guides on how different candidates voted on issues related to our biblical values. Then the women wore their red shoes to the polls and voted. I still like to wear red shoes to this day!

A main takeaway for the Deborahs United movement is that each woman can make a difference in her nation. This was shouted from the housetops in Taiwan, Indonesia, the United Kingdom, Hong Kong, Australia, and various other nations and states. The Company of Women in Latin America was hosted by Juanita Cercone of Enlace TV, and women from twenty-five nations attended. Top women leaders were knitted together in relationships that have lasted.

I encourage all readers (man or woman) to make a difference in the lives of your neighborhoods, cities, and nations. Each person was born for greatness, and you have an important place in God's divine plan.

15

The Dearest of Deborahs

One of the most influential and dearest to me among the Deborahs Company was my sister, Lucy Riethmiller. I mentioned in the previous chapter how she hosted a number of Deb Co meetings in Minnesota. One of my most painful experiences—yet also a time that resulted in some of the deepest life lessons I ever learned—involved Lucy. Frankly, it was hard to find a place in my story where I could relate this narrative and feel I was doing it justice, but it seems fitting to talk more about her among the Deborahs.

You might remember that I prophesied her birth when I was four. We were close—really close. Lucy was a bright beam of sunlight to all who knew her. Deeply generous and kind, she loved the poor and downtrodden. Her counseling knowledge brought healing to other people's souls and spirits.

When Lucy was fifty-one years old, she went to the eye doctor for a check-up. To her shock, the doctor found a tumor in her eye. Upon further evaluation, she was diagnosed with melanoma of the eye. Of course, this was deeply distressing to the whole family.

Lucy underwent surgery and radiation and came through both with flying colors, without any additional impact to her eye. It was amazing! We rejoiced, and it seemed as if she had come through unscathed. Six years later, however, she was tired all the time and seemed as though she could hardly make it through a day.

One day, Lucy called me from the airport in Minneapolis and said, "I am in such pain! It might be my heart."

She went to the emergency room to be checked out. To our horrible distress, the doctors said, "You are in late-stage cancer."

Cancer. That word. *Cancer.* I hate cancer. But we had seen people healed of cancer, so we had faith Lucy would be fine. At last, she and her husband, Mark, decided she should go to the most advanced place for treatment that they knew, the famous Mayo Clinic in Rochester, Minnesota.

After a battery of tests there, Lucy called me. "Cindy, the cancer is in my liver. It has metastasized in my body."

The Whole World Prayed

Initially, there was hope she could be a candidate for an ablation or for an experimental drug that had seen success. I did not realize, at the time, there was a zero recovery rate once melanoma cancer hit the liver. I flew out to Rochester to be with my sister. Everyone prayed. The whole world prayed. It seemed she had weeks to live.

I was staying in a small hotel room across the way from the hospital. The nighttimes were horrible. I cried and prayed. Lucy's church and friends prayed. Her best friend, Karen Kruger, came and stayed all night in the hospital, fasting and praying.

Healing did not come. Lucy died on July 2, 2012. I do not have words for the grief I felt. Frankly, I struggled whether to write about her death at all.

The real test of one's faith is not when things are going exactly the way you prayed for; the real test is what happens when it seems God did not heal and was silent. Lucy was a woman of great faith and had a lot to live for. Yet she was gone.

"Will You Give Your Sister to Me?"

My sister's funeral was a testament of a life lived brightly. Mark had a beautiful monarch butterfly put in the lid of his wife's casket. Many people testified of the change she had made to their lives. One man was deeply addicted and completely without hope, until she counseled him and he was completely freed.

I led worship that day. Lucy's funeral was on July 7. Planning her funeral around the same dates we had planned for my dad's was difficult. Double emotions ran through me. Yet I knew I needed to praise God through them and in spite of what had happened.

The week after Lucy's funeral, I was scheduled to preach in Bali, Indonesia. Up late one night, I went into the bathroom because Mike was sleeping. Grief clawed through me. I told the Lord, *I can't preach unless You do something for me.*

He quietly said, *You have a spirit of grief. Cast it out.*

I did. After that, I still grieved, but the wrenching pain was gone. The God of comfort was there for me.

As I processed through the grief, I felt the Lord say to me, *Cindy, can you trust Me even though this didn't turn out how you prayed? Even though it is a mystery to you now? Will you give your sister to Me? She is in heaven, fulfilling her calling.* The other thing He said to me was, *Cindy, you don't understand eternity at all! Heaven is not a punishment!*

Peace came with that as I cried out to God, "I do trust You, Lord!"

Holding Out or Leaping Out?

Months later, I was preaching at a convention center in Mexico when the Lord quietly said, *You are holding out on Me, Cindy. You have stopped praying for the sick.*

Had I changed my belief in healing? No. I knew the Bible promised that healing was the children's bread. I could not embrace and live by experiential theology, even in the midst of my great grief. By this, I mean I could not reject what the Bible says about healing—that we can be healed! Even though Lucy was not healed in this life, I still needed to believe in healing this side of heaven and live my life believing God is a healer.

Okay, Lord, I murmured internally, *I'm leaping out in faith again.* At that, I looked at a lady with a cane in the front row. I went up to her and took her hand and said, "Walk with me!" She got up and, hand-in-hand, we began to walk. She was hesitant at first, kind of limping along. And then I had the gift of faith well up in me and told her, "Now walk by yourself!" She did! In fact, she ended up running and was completely healed. Her cane became a relic of her past pain.

God doesn't just meet us on the mountaintops. He is there for us in the valleys—even the deep, dark ones.

A Prayer over Deep Grief

Let me pray with you:

> *Father, I thank You that we can trust You in life's mysteries, without letting them change the way we believe and shake our faith. You are a good, good God, and we thank You that You never change Your nature and character. We won't get shipwrecked in our faith in the midst of deep grief, even when we don't understand. In Jesus' name, Amen.*

As I have lived my life, one thing that has saved me in the middle of great trouble is coming to the realization that God is always there—fighting for me, helping me, and loving me. He will do the same for you, even in the middle of life's deepest sorrows or biggest challenges.

16

The Apostolic Council of Prophetic Elders

One of the biggest pioneering works we have done through the ministry is that I chair a movement of influential prophets. Earlier, I mentioned the Apostolic Council of Prophetic Elders (ACPE), established in 1999. Peter Wagner chose the name. As far as I know, it is the longest-running roundtable of prophets in the world.

Our ACPE group is not a top-down, vertical network, but rather a horizontal, covenantal, relational network. We are there for each other and truly love one another. Each year, we work together in November to get a corporate word for the coming year. Looking back at the track record of this group, we have been remarkably accurate. One year, we prophesied a virus would come that was seemingly incurable—and that turned out to be COVID.

As of this writing, we are a group of around seventy leaders. It is amazing how, as we get together to prophesy and pray, we work so well together. We know who specializes in what area. For instance, Sharon Stone and Arleen Westerhof host the European Roundtable of Prophets, and they are our specialists regarding Europe. Rick and Patricia Ridings have had a 24-7 prayer room in Jerusalem since 1999, and they know the inside workings of the Middle East and have hosted meetings of leaders in Dubai.

These regional and international roundtables are strategic in their time of prophesying and intercession. One held under a sanctioned church in Egypt was for a special time of intercession in the Middle East. During that time, the role of Egypt was highlighted, and we prayed about the connection between the United States, Egypt, President Trump, and President El-Sisi. Two weeks later, we watched as Egypt hosted the Gaza peace summit. Prayer works! Watchmen prophets are so critical in seeing God's will come to pass, and God listens when His people pray.

It is fascinating to work with prophets. I mentioned earlier that Peter Wagner used to say working with prophets was like herding cats. He would start our meetings with what he felt God was saying for the year, and then he never knew where the discussion would go after that! Somehow, it always turned out powerful, and God spoke to us corporately in a meaningful way.

ACPE's Miraculous Longevity

To keep a group of major leaders together for twenty-six years is really quite a miracle! It is unusual for a roundtable to last that long on any subject. It takes quite a bit of behind-the-scenes work, especially when various nations and continents are convening. This is because national politics and feelings can bleed into the meetings. Of course, no one wants this to happen, but we are all human.

The great thing is that the prophetic leaders in ACPE are so covenantal that there is an honoring of one another that transcends all those things. There were also times when we needed to understand why presidents and leaders of various nations were making decisions. We found the relationships among prophets also need to be tended to, just as with other types of leaders.

When ACPE began to meet, we agreed we would not speak against one another. As far as I know, this was only broken once, when someone came for a short time and criticized the group after the first meeting. That was a lesson for us, and it has not happened again. It is so special to meet with very visible leaders, authors, and speakers who defer to one another.

One time, one of the ACPE members told me about a Bible teacher who was speaking against me in a class and saying I was making outrageous demands. Among other things, this person claimed I demanded to be driven in a limousine before my speaking engagements. Indeed, this person had seen me arrive in a hired car—but it had been hired and paid for by someone else and was not a limousine. Being told about the accusation allowed me to quickly remedy a potentially damaging situation to my reputation.

The Global Prophetic Consultation

In 2017, James Goll, one of our prophetic elders and one of the original founders, gave a word during our meeting that I was to convene a group of international prophets in Dallas. I thought while listening to the word, *Oh my, that is going to be a lot of work!* And it has been! After that word, we founded the Global

Prophetic Consultation (GPC). I want to add that it has been quite rewarding for all of us to meet together.

How do you find prophets from around the world? We eventually invited leaders from sixty-five nations. The task of finding them has been an interesting journey. I would receive names from various people here at home, and when I followed up on the names by checking with spiritual leaders in those nations, sometimes they would say, "No! Don't invite that person! They use people financially." It has been a careful and thorough process, but we now invite up to three hundred leaders from various nations. Each is asked to bring a prophecy for the next year.

After all these years together, we have also become quite good friends. Many now preach for one another and are changing the world. We currently have roundtables for all of Europe, Australia, and other nations. In addition, we are hosting our first-ever roundtable in Cairo for the Middle East, and others for Asia and Africa.

In addition to the GPC roundtables, we also have those prophets who are invited to speak at the Global Prophetic Summit. These summits are powerful times when the prophets give the words they are receiving for the upcoming year.

Helping Define Prophetic Terms

With so much going on as ACPE and our roundtables were established, it seemed sensible to define the terms we were using so we would all be on the same page and people could gain a better understanding of the prophetic. Meeting together helped establish the language now used around the prophetic in our day.

In fact, in 1995 when I wrote *The Voice of God*, which was later abridged as a shorter version titled *The Essential Guide to the Prophetic*, it was probably only the third book written about the prophetic at that time. As far as I can track, John and Paula Sandford wrote *The Elijah Task* in 1977, and then Dr. Bill Hamon wrote *Prophets and Personal Prophecy* in 1987.

When I wrote *The Voice of God*, I used some terms that people were unfamiliar with, so the publisher asked me to define my terms right in the text to help people understand. Terms like *prophetic acts* might have been in use for the things that were happening, but people needed language that could be used across the board. So we started giving language to concepts such as prophetic intercession and prophetic praise. My mentor, Peter Wagner, was a master at coining words for movements, and I just followed in his footsteps. These days, the language of the prophetic is much more widely understood.

Prophets in Every Mountain

Our prophetic movement, like Bishop Hamon's, consists of watchman prophets. When we get a word of warning, we pray about it. I consider Dr. Hamon to be the father of the modern-day prophetic movement. He is one of the elders of the ACPE, along with the likes of Bishop Joseph Garlington. Earlier elders were John and Paula Sandford, and Sister Gwen Shaw, who established the End-Time Handmaidens. (By the way, you have to fast twenty-one days in order to join the Handmaidens.)

In 2015, when I started chairing the ACPE, I asked the group to send in names of young, emerging prophets, and we would add them to the roundtable. We have also been very intentional about making the group multiethnic. Many of these emerging prophets were just beginning when we heard about them, but now they are full-blown prophets and leaders. As Peter Wagner used to say, "There is no success without a successor."

When we started what became the ACPE, we knew of very few prophets around the world—not that God had not always been speaking, but most prophets did not know of each other. I remember a prophecy that Bill Hamon gave in the 1980s that there would one day be ten thousand prophets in the United States alone, and one hundred thousand around the world. In our first meeting, the majority were church prophets, and now we know there are prophets in every mountain or sphere of society.

Despite the growing size of our group, however, Peter taught me that for good group discussions, the numbers needed to be more like twelve, twenty-five, or fifty. We are past that limit of fifty in the ACPE since we added some regional leaders. But we are working to hold the line so we can still function as a prophetic dialogue group and facilitate our prophetic flow. One time, we started prophesying and went on for eight hours! It was glorious!

Each year, after the ACPE and the GPC meetings, I gather all of the prophecies from both groups and collate them into one document. It usually takes me around eight or more hours on the first round. Afterward, I send it to the ACPE to judge and see if they have anything to add. Then I rework it and send it to everyone to distribute to their networks. I have done this for around twenty years. Someday, hopefully, someone else will take up this job. The document for 2025 was fifteen pages long—the prophets really had a lot to say! I'm told many people use this document each year. We give it a theme and issue it as the word of the Lord for its specific year, and people use this combined word to pray and seek the Lord for direction in both their personal and corporate lives.

17

Spiritual Diplomacy and Protocol

Diplomacy: "the profession, activity, or skill of managing international relations, typically by a country's representatives abroad." It is "the art of dealing with people in a sensitive and effective way."*

As I have tried to make this memoir not just my story but also a mentoring resource, I am going to tackle a subject I have not heard widely taught—the subject of spiritual diplomacy and protocol.

"I have become all things to all men, that I might by all means save some" (1 Corinthians 9:22). Here, Paul is essentially talking about adapting to the culture of every place. *The Passion Translation* says it exactly like that: "I have adapted to the culture of every place I've gone so that I could more easily win people to Christ." Of course, that is never a license to sin! We must put the boundaries of the gospel around everything we say and do.

* *Oxford Languages Dictionary*, Google search result, "diplomacy," accessed February 2, 2026, https://www.google.com/search?q=diplomacy.

Protocol: "the official procedure or system of rules governing affairs of state or diplomatic occasions."*

When I lectured at Fuller Seminary for Dr. C. Peter Wagner, I learned about something called *contextualization*. Essentially, this means presenting the gospel in the context of the hearer. We can be guilty of bringing our cultural biases and attitudes into how we present the gospel.

I remember teaching in an Eastern European nation not many years after the fall of the Soviet Union. Afterward, a leader stopped and thanked me for not being a "typical American." I thanked him, but sensed there was something I needed to learn. He went on to say, "Most Americans come and talk down to us like we don't know anything. Many lecture us as if we have no spiritual understanding."

After this conversation, I pondered what I had heard. We Americans can be guilty of spiritual pride. In reality, those pastors who had lived under terrible threats, failings, and persecution were deeply spiritual students of the Word. Americans have a lot to learn from them. Contextualization, therefore, needs to become part of our protocol. Those of us from the United States who minister internationally can avoid being "typical Americans" by honoring our hosts in our presentations and acknowledging their giftedness and depth of knowledge.

Using Interactive Preaching and Filters

In a more general sense, I find one of the greatest ways to reach the heart of an audience is through what I call *interactive preaching*.

* *Oxford Languages Dictionary*, Google search result, "protocol," accessed February 2, 2026, https://www.google.com/search?q=protocol.

What do I mean by that? I ask the audience rhetorical questions. Rhetoric is the art of persuasive speaking or writing.

For instance, you might ask your listeners questions like these: "What do I do?" "Why are these bad things happening to me?" You're anticipating the audience's questions. You can also preach interactively through a form of a word of knowledge, by expressing what the Holy Spirit shows you the audience may be feeling. This shows empathy and that you care about what they're going through.

We can learn to be spiritually adept in the way we speak, write, text, and communicate with others. This involves developing filters. Before you communicate with someone, think about who they are. What is their culture? What position do they hold in relation to yours? How much honor should you give? For instance, when speaking to a leader, always use his or her proper title. Also, never call government officials by their first name unless they've given you permission—especially not in public.

The Importance of Honor

Honor is extremely important in all communication. It's a biblical principle that is not commonly understood. In many cultures, honor is so interwoven into the society that you can easily offend someone through your words or even body language. In some cultures, one must not look a king or ruler in the eye; your eyes must be downcast. When in a new setting, observe how others behave and how they address the person of honor.

"Honor the Lord with your possessions, and with the firstfruits of all your increase; so your barns will be filled with plenty, and your vats will overflow with new wine" (Proverbs 3:9–10). Spiritual diplomacy must include our interactions with God.

He is preeminent. How we address and honor Him in our daily lives is critical.

I even see Christians using the Lord's name in vain online—posting things like "OMG," a shortened form of "Oh my God!" (the expression *not* meant as a prayer). One time on a plane, a man was swearing using Jesus' name. I said, "Look, my name is Cindy. If you must swear, use my name instead of God's." He stopped.

"Honor your father and your mother, as the LORD your God has commanded you, that your days may be long, and that it may be well with you in the land which the LORD your God is giving you" (Deuteronomy 5:16). I often notice it when people don't honor their parents in their speech. It reveals they don't understand the blessing that comes with honor. God does not take lightly the dishonoring of parents. Even if your parents have been abusive, honor them to the extent you can—without allowing them to take advantage of you.

Another way to bestow honor is by blessing your pastors and spiritual leaders. Those who have never been in a leadership role have no idea how difficult it can be. Pastors listen to people's problems, pray for their families, and show up in crises—this can be a heavy burden. A simple note of appreciation can be priceless.

Some people resist a spiritual "culture of honor" because they fear it silences victims of clergy abuse. I recommend building safeguards into the culture—openly stating that if anyone is being abused, there is a safe and confidential way to report it. Using Matthew 18:15 to require a victim to confront a leader one-on-one can be damaging—especially in cases of sexual abuse. Every ministry should have a trusted person or committee to receive reports and deal with leadership issues. Unfortunately, some ministries "circle the wagons" and protect the institution at all costs. In those cases, I suggest you contact a local pastor for support.

Everyone needs someone to be accountable to! Mike and I attend Trinity Church in Cedar Hill, Texas, and we are accountable there. Every traveling minister needs a local pastor and church.

Some Important Protocols

When Mike and I meet with a head of state, we're often given a protocol briefing. For instance, they might give you a strict time limit. Never break that—try to end early. (By the way, I tell public speakers the same: Always give the mic back a little early. It shows humility and respect for the schedule.)

As a prophet to nations, I have found that many people don't understand protocol, and it leaves a bad impression—despite the legitimacy of their message. For example, some people bring shofars and blow them loudly or act overly dramatic. Our prayer network, the Reformation Prayer Network, has hosted meetings at the US Capitol, and nearly every time, I've had to apologize for someone's behavior—whether they anointed government buildings with oil or got arrested.

When speaking to elected officials, keep your tone conversational. You might say, "Here's something I'd like you to consider." If the official is a Christian and charismatic, and you know them well, you can be more direct.

Deference: "respectful submission or yielding to the judgment, will, opinion, etc., of another." It is "respectful or courteous regard."*

* *Dictionary.com*, "deference," accessed February 2, 2026, https://www.dictionary.com/browse/deference.

Deference is essential when talking to an elder, parent, pastor, or leader of any kind. In written communication, applying deference is especially challenging. When you're upset, it's easy to be direct, but that can come across as scolding or accusatory. Instead, try saying, "This situation is happening, and I feel something should be done. Perhaps this could be a good solution," rather than "You did this" or "You never do that."

Written communication lacks tone and body language, so it almost always feels harsher than intended.

If you're upset, write your first draft and ask yourself, *Will this sound as though I'm not showing deference? Am I just venting?* One time, a liberal news commentator did a hit piece on me. I wrote a response, but then I felt the Lord say, *Do you feel better now? Good. Now don't send it.*

Give your writing a pause until your emotions settle. Were you triggered? Why did you write it? Another wise move is to send it to a trusted friend for feedback. "In the multitude of counselors there is safety" (Proverbs 11:14).

Texting uses fewer words, so kindness matters even more. I learned the "sandwich method" from my mentor, Peter Wagner: Start with encouragement, then state the correction, and close with another encouraging word.

Before correcting someone, ask yourself, *Am I the right person to do this?* Suggest rather than instruct, unless you're in a clear position of authority. And always take it to prayer. If it's an abusive situation, involve someone else.

In an email, notice how someone signs off. The person might start the email as "Bishop," but close it with "Pastor Fred"—giving you permission to address him differently.

When communicating with someone under your leadership, open a correction with, "Help me understand what's going on with . . ." Then listen. The person's response may reveal something you didn't know, which will shape your communication.

If you're a speaker or minister, always use the appropriate title for the senior leader of the church. Every ministry has its own culture. Some use first names, while others expect formal titles.

Women leaders can unintentionally offend male pastors by delivering direct prophetic words without context. If you don't know the person well, say something like, "Here's something I feel I'm hearing from the Lord. I'd love your thoughts." That way, you're not dropping a "Thus says the Lord" bomb without giving the person time to process.

As relationships grow, you can be more direct. But never try to correct a pastor's congregation with a word unless you've run it by the pastor. And a word like "You're exhausted and need a sabbatical" should be delivered privately—even if it's accurate.

Even within the United States, communication styles vary widely. In the South (including Texas), people tend to be more indirect—you're expected to greet someone, ask about his or her family, and then get to the point. In places like New York or New Jersey, people often prefer you skip the pleasantries and be direct. In some cultures, people never make a direct request. They'll say, "How are you?" and leave it at that. You're supposed to follow up.

Always consider whom you're speaking to and what their cultural background is. When in doubt, use deference. Even teenagers should be communicated with in a way that honors them. They have feelings too!

At our conferences, we interact with many cultures. Despite our best efforts, we sometimes miss a boundary. I'm always trying to grow in communication and cultural understanding.

18

On Being a Prophet

I told you about how I first prophesied when I was four years old, telling my mom that I was going to have a baby sister. She smiled with that halfway look parents sometimes give when they don't believe their child.

I used to tease Lucy that I had prepared the way for her so she wouldn't feel rejected. Then I did that "big sister" thing where I said, "So you owe me chocolate and shoes!" (She was so generous that I didn't have to ask!)

I think if I had grown up in a charismatic/Pentecostal church, it might have been a bit easier for me to find my way into being a prophet. But our denomination believed the gifts had passed away with the last apostle, so at times I just felt weird.

Prophets can be strange at times anyway, though. Even I think I am rather strange myself. One moment I'm cleaning my bathtub, and the next I'm writing a government leader with a word. Unusual, huh? Not your everyday life!

Prophetic Words for Presidents

One time, we were eating Mexican food with leaders from an African nation. I looked up at our friends and said, "You know the president of the nation, don't you? Call him and tell him that the military is planning a coup!" I then went back to eating chips and salsa.

See what I mean? The rest of the story is that they did warn the president, and the military was planning a coup, but they were able to stop it because of the warning. (Of course, our friends prayed too.) Just another day in the life of a prophet to nations!

Another time I went to see the president of a different African nation. While waiting to see the president, I saw a man dressed all in white standing in the anteroom. The Lord said to me, *That man is planning a coup against the president.*

I asked who he was and learned he was the vice president. I told the president, "Your vice president is planning a coup." Later, the VP was caught escaping the country with a large sum of money in his suitcase. The coup didn't materialize because the leader had been warned.

A Prophet to Nations

How did I know I was called to be a prophet to nations? That is a good question. For one, I gravitate toward prophesying over nations and government officials. Of course, it wasn't that way in the beginning; I grew into it.

I only have to listen to other prophets and watch their prophetic track record to see where they align in their prophetic gift. Some, like my dear friend Bishop Bill Hamon, are church prophets. He is one of those, by his own admission. That doesn't mean he doesn't prophesy over nations, but it is not the usual for him.

A prophet to nations will have Jeremiah 1:8–10 resonate in his or her heart:

> "Do not be afraid of their faces, for I am with you to deliver you," says the LORD. Then the LORD put forth His hand and touched my mouth, and the LORD said to me: "Behold, I have put My words in your mouth. See, I have this day set you over the nations and over the kingdoms, to root out and to pull down, to destroy and to throw down, to build and to plant."

A prophet to nations is almost always a watchman prophet. By this, I mean that prophets to nations will give a word, and then God will also give them a strategy to pray over that word. The word might come with a warning. This warning is not fate. There will be a strategy that a merciful God will give to counteract it; otherwise, why does He warn?

It is our job as prophets not only to listen to hear from God what the judgment is to come, or even what the devil is trying to do, but to either petition the Lord or find out what is causing the judgment. What needs to be repented of? Some prophets only prophesy out of the second heavens, or what the devil is doing, but don't seek the solutions from the third heaven, where God's throne is, for the strategy on how to pray. In order to have a fuller understanding of how to pray, please read my first book, *Possessing the Gates of the Enemy*.

Staying Emotionally Whole

One of the important things a prophet must work on is staying emotionally whole. In the 1980s, I got hold of books on inner healing by John and Paula Sandford. They later became our dear friends and are now in heaven. They were pioneers on the subject and took a lot of persecution for it. I learned so much from the Sandfords and spent quality time processing through my life. As the child of a church-planting mom and dad, I had some pain and rejection. It seems that if people can't get to the pastor with their complaints, they like to dump on his children.

By the way, this has also happened to my own children. One time while I was preaching at a large church, the pastor took my eight-year-old son aside and said, "Tell me, do you really like your mama being a woman minister?" I was so upset when Daniel told me that!

All leaders and ministers need to be emotionally whole, but I feel prophets especially need to work on it because it can affect how they prophesy. I have heard prophets who have a bias against another nation prophesy an inaccurate word because they were tainted by the news from their own nations. They tapped into the news of the day rather than God's news. A friend of mine moved to America and later told me, "I have a completely different view of the US now that I live here, rather than listening to BBC and CNN International news!" Of course, Americans can also misjudge another nation in the same way.

Daily forgiveness is an important part of being whole. Forgive those who have hurt your family or those you love. One can pick up an offense of another person, and it isn't yours to carry! There doesn't seem to be the same grace when you pick up an offense as when someone offends you directly.

During that season before our marriage when I lived at home and had broken up with Mike, I made lists of people I needed to forgive. A lot of my offenses were things people had done to my preacher daddy or my mama. Church hurt made up a big part of my forgiving and asking God to restore my soul (see Psalm 23:3). Our emotional or soul realm can be quite damaged, but I have found that God is quite good at healing my hurt and taking my pain. Jesus bore our sorrows on the cross (see Isaiah 53:4).

There are so many avenues one can use to get inner healing today. It's always good to have an outside voice. If you are married, a spouse can be valuable to let you know you could use some prayer. Develop prayer partners who love you and whom you can ask about your emotional health as well. I have seen people get hurt and start "leaking" emotionally all over social media. This causes others to have to choose sides. (Of course, in the case of clergy abuse, this seems to have been the only recourse for some whistle-blowers.)

I have often said if you are called to ministry, you can't wear your emotions on your sleeve. One needs to have the hide of a rhinoceros and the heart of a dove! One should not "prophesy" from a place of rejection. God is very good at fighting our battles. As I look back over my life, He has fought for me many times—even though it has often taken years.

Becoming Adept at Your Prophetic Gift

As you progress as a prophet, you can become more adept at using your gift. A prophetic word can contain various gifts being manifested—for instance, a word of knowledge for healing. Other times, it will be a word of wisdom for something in a person's future. It used to be, I am told, that in Pentecostal circles, they taught that God would never prophesy anything future that you do not already have knowledge about. This is not true! One of the powerful uses of the prophetic gift is to prophesy about a person's future destiny. I experienced this when an old-time prophet, Dick Mills, prophesied I would have a worldwide ministry. At that time, I had spoken in only one nation other than my own, Canada. (Read more about the prophetic gift in my book *The Essential Guide to the Prophetic.*) The New Testament talks about future famines, how Paul was prophetically warned about going to Rome, and many other future things.

One time I was prophesying over a woman and suddenly said, "Call your husband and tell him to go to the emergency room right now!"

She called him, and he replied, "I don't even feel sick!" However, at the word of the Lord, he went. Doctors found that he was hemorrhaging internally, and it saved his life.

19

Healing of the Land

One of the foundational calls of Generals International is to heal nations. I wrote extensively in *Possessing the Gates of the Enemy* about how to heal nations. However, there are stories of dramatic changes to nations that I think are important to share in my memoirs. Revelation 22:1–2 (NIV, emphasis added) says,

> And he showed me a pure river of water of life, clear as crystal, proceeding from the throne of God and of the Lamb. In the middle of its street, and on either side of the river, was the tree of life, which bore twelve fruits, each tree yielding its fruit every month. The leaves of the tree were for the *healing of the nations.*

The scriptural placement of this passage is important. I used to assume this was a picture of the sweet by-and-by and a future dispensation. However, notice there is a time stamp in the passage—it refers to the fruit yield happening *every month*, so it cannot be referring to the future, when time will be no more. This is a huge scriptural understanding. The very last chapter of the Bible says that nations can be healed and there is provision for it.

As a prophet of governments and nations, I take the job of healing nations very seriously. As we look around the world today, we can see our cities are very sick, troubled, and in need of healing. As an intercessor, my mandate is to use 2 Chronicles 7:14, and train others to do so, in a way that sees God moving to bring nations back to their created mandate: "If My people who are called by My name will humble themselves, and pray and seek My face, and turn from their wicked ways . . . I will . . . heal their land."

It's fascinating that the word *heal* here is from the Hebrew word *rapha*, which is the same word in God's name Jehovah Rapha, meaning the Lord who heals. While this book relates my memoirs and is not meant to be a teaching manual as much as my other books, let me give you some instances where we have seen remarkable healing of the nations through prayer.

Fishing in Fiji

Fiji is a stunning nation surrounded by beautiful waters. When I first went to minister there, I prophesied that a nation from the East would build a sports stadium for them and that it would be used for the preaching of the gospel. China did come and build a stadium, and Reinhard Bonnke was the first to preach there.

The next time I visited Fiji, the minister of fisheries came to me with a problem. Their waters were being fished out by foreign entities. She asked me what to do, to which I replied, "You are the governmental representative for the waters. You can bring healing."

She asked, "How do I do it?"

I said, "There were many pirates who used these waters and brought sexual sin and other breaking of the law to this land. Go to the water, take your shoes off, wade into the water, and pray this: 'Father God, I now repent of the sin of piracy done in these waters, and of the sexual sin and breaking of laws. I now break the curses released into these waters.'"

She did so, and said afterward, "We still don't have the fish!"

To which I replied, "God hasn't stopped being the creator. He will just make more." And He did!

I found out later that people who worked with George Otis Jr.'s International Fellowship of Transformation Partners has also sent out healing-the-land teams.

What happened after that? Various coral reefs that had been dying started living again. Fish of a kind the nation had not seen in years were found in abundance. Not only that, but they started finding an abundance of a special type of seashell they had only previously heard of. Other intercessors started praying at other spots around the nation, and I heard that George Otis Jr. was also teaching there on transformation. It all worked together for good!

The "Desert of Death" Comes to Life

One of the most dramatic stories occurred in a part of Pakistan known as the "Desert of Death." A Presbyterian missionary had heard me teach at Fuller Seminary on healing the land. He was working in a largely unreached people group in this Desert of Death area at the time, with not much success. He had purchased a piece of land in the desert for a Bible training center.

After he heard the teaching, he went back and wrote Scriptures on wooden stakes and drove them into the ground on the four corners of his training center. He then prayed, "This land belongs to the Kingdom of God. I now repent of the sin of idolatry, and witchcraft, sexual sin, and any other sin against God. I now break the curses that have come from this sin and pray blessings over this property." (This was according to Hosea 4:1–3; 2 Chronicles 7:14; Leviticus 18:25.)

The missionary then drilled a well and tapped into an underground river of sweet drinking water! The only sweet water in the area. He planted a number of little seedling trees known for their land-healing properties, and in two years they grew as large as twenty-five-year-old trees. The locals called it a miracle! From that time, this missionary made wonderful advances for the Kingdom of God.

Sweet Water Surfaces in Argentina

The last story I will include here took place in Northern Argentina, in the Chaco province. The native people of the area had been slaughtered by the Spanish conquerors. The area where they were killed became sacred to the remaining native people. Sadly, the curse that worked in the land also worked even in the water table, as it reversed and went underground, leaving only stagnant water on the surface.

Eduardo Lorenzo, one of Argentina's great spiritual leaders who is now with the Lord, was of Spanish descent. He repented to the natives of the sins of the Spanish conquerors through identificational repentance, and they forgave.

The intercessors then went to the sacred site and prayed, asking God to heal the land. It worked! The land stopped mourning (see Hosea 4), and the water table reversed so that the water on top became sweet to drink again.

The Land Can Rejoice Again!

To the Western mind, the cause and effect of such prayer for healing of the land seems impossible, or improbable at the least. However, God's promise to heal the land is true, and when applied, the land begins to rejoice! (For a more detailed biblical explanation of this, see my book *Deliver Us from Evil*.)

We have seen areas under severe drought where, as God restored the land, it started to rain again and the harvest was three times the normal bounty! The president of Kenya led a prayer of repentance when there was severe drought, and the nation prayed together and repented of its sin. Then the rain came and healed the land.

The sin of the people causes the land to become sick. King David realized this had happened when the nation of Israel faced three successive years of drought (see 2 Samuel 21:1–2). God healed the land when blood was shed. Thank God that the shedding of blood has already been done for us on the cross, and we can repent and see our nations healed!

It is absolutely essential to understand that we are supernatural and the mandate God gave us at our creation to steward the land has never ceased to be part of our job description. In other words, God created us to take care of His creation, and we do it by prayer. I love seeing nations healed and the barren places restored.

20

Generals International

As I mentioned earlier, we changed the name of the ministry from Generals of Intercession to Generals International in 2003, although a number of our friends still call us Generals of Intercession. Today, we have the Reformation Prayer Network in all fifty states, and it's divided into fourteen regions. Thank God for our dear friend and staff member Timmerle Kelly, who keeps it running smoothly and takes on a large workload to keep things going.

While I have already written a bit about the ministry of GI, I would like to amplify it in this chapter. First of all, why do we call the members generals? Because God called us to gather "the generals" to pray for America in 1984. I had initially posed a question to the Lord: *Why has Satan been able to make so much progress in the United States with his agenda?*

As often seems to happen, I received a commissioning that Mike and I—as we are one—have done our best to follow. The Lord said, *Satan has a strategy, and My people do not. Call together the generals to pray, and I will reveal a strategy to heal the nation. Call them to repent for the sins of the nation.*

We now know this is called identificational repentance, and it is based on 2 Chronicles 7:14, which I quoted in the previous chapter. But let's look at it again: "If My people who are called by My name will humble themselves, and pray and seek My face, and turn from their wicked ways . . . I will . . . heal their land."

Identificational repentance seems like nothing new to us today, but at the time the Lord commissioned us, it was revolutionary. I remember meeting my friend John Dawson after this encounter, and he said God was speaking the same thing to him. In fact, he's the one who coined the term *identificational repentance* and wrote about it in his excellent books *Taking Our Cities for God* and *Healing America's Wounds*. I also write about this extensively in my first book, *Possessing the Gates of the Enemy*.

I remember asking the Lord during that encounter, *What are the sins of my nation?* He went on to show me our sin of enslaving Africans, the horrific Trail of Tears, and the killing of Native Americans. Other sins included putting Japanese and Italians in internment camps during World War II.

We held our first GI meeting at Church on the Rock in Rockwall, Texas. I called around and spoke to ministries in the Dallas–Fort Worth area to ask if they would send their prayer leaders. I found only two ministries that had designated prayer leaders—Kenneth Copeland Ministries and our host church. However, several churches sent a representative. We probably had around ten ministries represented in our first meeting to pray for the nation together.

That first meeting was so powerful, although even in the charismatic community there were divisions in beliefs around such things as deliverance and suffering. Yet we all knew we had to come to the foot of the cross to cry out for the nation. The first meeting began a round of meetings where different ministries hosted monthly gatherings. God met us, and lasting friendships ensued.

What Is a General?

In military terms, a general is a high-ranking official responsible for commanding a large group of soldiers. In the church world, the term is used more loosely—a general is someone with the gift of leadership who leads groups in prayer. These spiritual generals are often noted for their ability to withstand great pressure, and at times persecution.

It surprised Mike and me that we got so much guff about naming the ministry Generals of Intercession. We had originally started as Crown of Glory Ministries, but after we had a couple of meetings with the generals, everyone just started calling us Generals of Intercession. We received letters from India and the United Kingdom claiming it was too audacious a name and inferring that we thought much higher of ourselves than we ought.

Mike and I prayed about changing the name but felt that—similar to the name The Salvation Army that people also took exception to—we would outlast the criticism. And it has proven to be true.

Themes of Repentance

The GI meetings in various places would have a theme of something we felt needed to be repented of there. For instance, the meetings in Tulsa, hosted at the Mabee Center at Oral Roberts

University, involved the city's different ministries repenting of their disunity and lack of cooperation.

The exciting part of these meetings was the great fruit we saw from our times of identificational repentance. After our prayer time at ORU, at the International Charismatic Bible Ministries conference held there, Dr. Yonggi Cho publicly repented to Kenneth Copeland for not hosting him due to negative opinions. I sat and watched that moment unfold from the nosebleed section and marveled at the power of prayer.

Another significant answer to prayer came after we repented with a group of leaders in 1987 in Pasadena, California, for the taking of property from Japanese Americans during World War II and for their internment. We asked God to move Congress to issue a proclamation of repentance. The Civil Liberties Act of 1988 provided a formal apology and a payment of $20,000 to those who were unjustly interned during WWII—a historic answer to prayer!

In 1987, we went to England to reconcile our grievances from the Revolutionary War. Initially, we had no contacts there, until we met our friends Rod and Julie Anderson, whom I mentioned earlier. At the time, Mike was working for American Airlines, so we flew stand-by on passes, which helped us considerably.

Faith Is Always in the Red

We have found that faith is always in the red—meaning God will ask us to do bigger and bigger things that we don't yet have the money for. When Mike left the airlines, where he forecasted multimillion-dollar budgets, we had some tense moments. He would look at what I had vision for and say, "We can't do that; we don't have the money!" Of course, he was right. But he quickly shifted to forecasting faith budgets—and God was always faithful to meet them.

Mike and I are a team. Generals International would not be a worldwide ministry without him. We bounce vision off each other and dream together. At times, we haven't agreed on what to do, but thank God for our board of directors and friends, who helped us. Accountability is essential, and every ministry must have it.

In my nearly fifty years of ministry, I have learned a thing or two—and Mike and I have learned many lessons about working together. There is an art to running a ministry. Some will always be mom-and-pop operations because they don't plan for expansion with staffing or they're afraid to take on big projects. Others lack the emotional and spiritual intelligence to grow, especially in terms of cross-cultural communications.

Marrying Prayer and Praise

One of our big projects was A Marriage of Prayer and Praise in 1986. I wrote about this in chapter 13, "Intercessory Praise," in *Possessing the Gates of the Enemy*. We were given a vision to hold a meeting in Washington, DC, where we would "marry" prayer and praise as a prophetic act. We even used a bridal canopy like what is used in Jewish weddings. The intercessors were on one side, the worship leaders on the other. They met in the middle, and we all danced together.

Putting on the meeting was rough. First, the leaders in DC told us stories about others who had tried to hold meetings there and failed—not encouraging! Second, the hotel wouldn't give us a contract without permission from the leaders of the Worship Symposium with Maranatha Music, because their event ended on Friday night and they didn't want a second worship event to detract from the first one. We didn't even know the conveners of this other event, so we flew to meet them, and they graciously agreed. They spoke to the hotel, and we got our contract.

I wanted to rent a small room, but Mike said we should get the ballroom. It was expensive and a huge stretch of faith! Only half of it was available, but Mike had them write into the contract that if the other party canceled, we'd get the whole space for the same amount. That's exactly what happened—and we filled it.

We didn't have a worship leader or many other pieces that we needed in place for the event to happen, so Mike and I got up at five every morning to pray before he went to work at seven. We did this for months ahead of time—and it bore great fruit.

The week of the meeting finally came. The same pastor who told us not to come offered his church's sound system and contacts. We met Tom Hess, who now leads All Nations Convocation in Jerusalem, and Jim Gilbert, who later wrote "I Love You with the Love of the Lord." A pastor brought her orchestra, and a woman from a famous Christian dance company brought her banners. God put it all together through five a.m. prayer!

Another large worship conference took place at the old PTL grounds in Fort Mill, South Carolina. We gathered worship leaders from many states for intercessory prayer in 1987. The Lord gave me the second week of July for the meeting. When I flew out to PTL to book the ballroom, they said, "Nobody gets it in July—we do dinner theater."

I replied, "Put us down as backup in case anything cancels." A week before our event, scandal hit PTL, and all dinner theaters were canceled. The staff appreciated our support, and we worshiped with all our hearts!

The financial side of ministry can also be challenging. We were growing rapidly and had about seven staff members. Bills always seemed to chase us. Mike and I went without a salary for six months once, but somehow, we made it. We always paid our staff, even when we weren't getting paid. They didn't know—we just did it. As I said, you can't grow without staff.

Prayer Journeys to the Nations

Another part of GI's ministry vision was prayer journeys—God-given assignments to go to specific nations. One of the first prayer journeys was to Vietnam to pray for healing from the war and for our soldiers.

That war deeply affected our generation. One of Mike's friends got into LSD while in Vietnam and later died by suicide. Many soldiers never really came home. They needed spiritual healing as well as physical. We learned from Point Man International Ministries that soldiers had been cursed from a place called the Marble Mountains in Da Nang—curses of homelessness, suicide, etc. We went to break those curses and pray.

We began in Washington, DC, at the Pentagon, with a team of five—including Chuck Pierce, who was a great help to me. Mike stayed home for work. We were given camouflage-covered New Testaments like the ones handed out in Vietnam. Then we visited the Vietnam War Memorial. We'd been told many soldiers had died by suicide during and after the war. Numbers vary, but some say more than 90,000. As I walked alongside that black wall, grief overwhelmed me, and tears poured down. Over 58,000 US soldiers died in that war. I don't know how many Vietnamese lives were lost.

Then we went to Vietnam, where our team would climb one of the Marble Mountains to pray. That morning, a maid banged on Chuck's door, warning the city would flood. We were on an upper floor, so we stood on a balcony and commanded the river to recede—and it did! People waved at us from boats as we prayed. Within an hour the streets were clear. We got in a van and went to the mountain.

We ended our trip in Ho Chi Minh City, praying for our soldiers and their remains to be brought home. At the War Remnants Museum there, we saw jars containing deformed babies affected by Agent Orange. We wept. The head of the museum noticed and invited us for tea. The next day's newspaper headline read "A Beautiful Apology." We weren't there to debate the war's validity, but to address the pain that followed. The famous photo of Phan Thi Kim Phúc, the little girl burned by napalm, was front and center in the museum. She later became a Christian and credits her faith with helping her move forward.

In the San Francisco Airport on our way home, we repented for how our nation treated returning soldiers. Today, many publicly thank service members.

Prayer journeys test your faith and endurance. The enemy doesn't want his kingdom undermined. There is also navigating unknown situations and spiritual diplomacy, as we talked about in an earlier chapter.

In October 2001, shortly after 9/11, Peter Wagner held Gideon's Army II in Hanover, Germany. Leaders from many nations came to pray. We Americans were raw. One leader unknowingly placed an American flag on the ground—which nearly caused an uproar. In the United States, the flag symbolizes those who have died defending it. Most nations have flag protocols; intercessors should be aware and respectful.

On every prayer journey, I build in fun bonding moments. For this team, we visited the Hanover Zoo before leaving for Russia—what a joy! The next morning, I told the team, "Now I'm General Cindy. From here on out, we work as a team. No wandering off. I don't want anyone arrested for taking a side trip."

In Russia, we planned to pray for healing from World War II. When we landed in St. Petersburg, the US State Department had just issued a travel warning for Russia. We prayed and felt peace to continue our journey, but we stayed alert. My book *Possessing the Gates of the Enemy* had already been translated and was being used across Russia by prayer teams.

News of my visit reached Igor Nikitin's church. I prophesied they would start Russian-speaking Christian television—and he later founded TBN Russia and helped launch TBN Shalom in Jerusalem.

Our last stop was Volgograd—formerly Stalingrad. The six-month battle there (August 1942 through February 1943) was one of the bloodiest in history. There were more than 1.1 million Allied casualties, and estimates for the Axis casualties range from 647,000 to nearly 1 million. Of 91,000 German POWs, only about 6,000 survived. Women helped defend the city, which was reduced to rubble.

To our surprise, we were greeted at the Volgograd airport by local pastors. They had maps and spiritual insight ready. I even spoke at a cultural hall once used by Communists—with paintings of Lenin above!

Hotels were unpredictable then. That first night, prostitutes relentlessly called our rooms. We implemented a buddy system to protect our team. The next morning, a grizzled man who carried our bags spoke English and asked to join us. He had spent his life digging graves for the war dead. We invited him to come with us.

James Goll, ever the joker, had the team count off military-style as we assembled, "Number one, reporting for duty! Number two, reporting for duty!" It brought levity to a heavy day.

At the battlefield, I picked up shrapnel. The ground still told its story. God whispered, *Ask the Russians to forgive the Germans.* I hesitated. He said, *Ask them to do it in the name of their lost loved ones.*

One by one, the Russians did so: "In the name of my grandfather, I forgive . . ."

The gravedigger watched, astonished. "I could not conceive how they could forgive the unforgivable," he said.

I explained, "These men can forgive because Jesus forgave them." I asked if he wanted to know Jesus, and with tears, he said yes.

Generals International has pioneered many movements—some lasting for years, some still ongoing. Deborahs Company and the Apostolic Council of Prophetic Elders still exist. In the next chapter, I'll share more on nations and prayer.

21

Asking for Nations

When I accepted the call to preach, one Scripture verse repeatedly jumped out at me: "Ask of Me, and I will give You the nations for Your inheritance, and the ends of the earth for Your possession" (Psalm 2:8).

I was in the parking lot of a California church in 1983 when I received a prophecy that I would go to many nations. *Nations?* I thought. *I've only been to Canada and on a tourist trip across the US border to Mexico!* But now, after traveling to many nations, I can see that was truly a word for my life. It also made sense because of my love for that particular verse.

The call to the nations is interesting. I can be completely jet-lagged and exhausted after a trip, thinking, *Let the younger ones do this kind of travel now*. Then one week later, I'll be looking at invitations to the ends of the earth! I once told someone, "I don't want therapy for that—it's just in me!"

Today, more than forty years after receiving that word, the call to the nations still burns inside me. It's like fire shut up in my bones! In the Bible the prophet Jeremiah describes it this way: "Then I said, 'I will not make mention of Him, nor speak anymore in His name.' But His word was in my heart like a burning fire shut up in my bones; I was weary of holding it back, and I could not" (Jeremiah 20:9).

Different Aspects of the Prophetic

There are different ministry gifts through which God will give a call to the nations. Some will do stadium events, using their gift of prophetic evangelism to win the lost and host healing meetings. I have flowed in that realm, and I love it! Soul-winning is in my bones. However, there still aren't many prophets to the nations. That is a different aspect of the prophetic. It requires not only prophetic gifting but also spiritual protocol to serve effectively as an ambassador of the Lord to presidents and government leaders.

I recently spoke at Christ For The Nations on the topic "Choosing to Be a Pioneer." In preparation, I looked up the statistics on unreached people groups in the world. According to the Joshua Project, as of this writing there are 7,188 unreached people groups—roughly 42 percent of the world's population.* It is my personal conviction that we must do more to reach them. Brave missionaries and Bible translators are still giving their lives to go where others will not—unsung heroes and heroines of the faith.

Every person who loves Jesus must engage in spreading the gospel—whether through prayer, through financial support, or by going themselves. I often say, "We need to stop taking water to the ocean and start taking it to the desert."

* For more on this, see the Joshua Project's website, especially the people groups' Global Dashboard page at https://joshuaproject.net/people_groups/dashboard.

Controversy or Cookies?

Pioneering doesn't stop with age—it only grows richer. One day I said to the Lord, *I'm tired of being controversial. Couldn't You have made me someone who just baked cookies for the women's group at church?*

I think I heard Him chuckle as He answered, *Cindy, you are always going to be controversial. The controversy of today is the commonplace of tomorrow. Just be obedient.*

I responded, *Yes, Lord, I will go.*

Today, with social media and the internet, it's even easier to become a target of accusations and slander. You have to work at keeping your heart right. I keep a list of those who have accused me of being a false prophet, and I bless them by name in my private devotions. This spiritual exercise keeps my heart pure.

Even criticism can make you better, as it forces you to examine whether there is any truth in it. Sometimes there's a kernel of truth that can help you grow. "All things work together for good to those who love God, to those who are the called according to His purpose" (Romans 8:28).

I remember Peter Wagner once said about people who often come under attack, "Cindy, watch those who get defensive and start answering their accusers. In my experience, their ministries often spiral downward afterward." I've had moments when I've come close to doing that myself.

One of the greatest blessings I have is Mike, along with my son, Daniel, and his wife, Jenay. Mike and my family have often quietly handled false accusations without my ever knowing. Once, however, I had to report a threatening text I received in Arabic, which a friend translated for me.

Seasoning Well with the Holy Spirit

Our lives, under the guidance of the Holy Spirit, should season well. With each season, we should become more Christlike. That should be a given—but it's good to evaluate ourselves regularly.

Over the years, I have worked on my ministry style to better follow the Holy Spirit's lead in meetings. I also have realized women's voices, in general, can be more strident, so I intentionally lower my pitch by about four notes. It helps, especially when I'm publicly prophesying and tend to get loud. I used to have a thick Texas accent that was difficult for translators, so I've worked on softening it. I remember once taking someone with a heavy Southern accent to Argentina, and my friend asked, "What did she say? I couldn't understand a word!"

It's also good to examine ourselves to avoid drifting into a backslidden state. One spiritual exercise I practice is checking whether I have been unloving during the day. I have had to go back and apologize to my staff after doing this—sometimes privately, sometimes publicly—because of my attitude.

At times I read 1 Corinthians 13, often called the Love Chapter, and realize I've fallen short. When one writes a memoir, you begin to assess your life. It has been much harder to write my story than I imagined. (Not to mention carving out the time!) I was surprised to find that I needed to go back and forgive—not just others but also myself. There are certain betrayals and disappointments I haven't written about because of the pain it would cause others. It has been more important to keep my heart right and focus on the great joys and miraculous victories God has given us along the way.

Pressing On in Faith to Grow

Very few ministers last more than forty years and continue to grow. It requires faith. The economy fluctuates, and each season demands new strategies. The stress of maintaining a staff can wear on you, so having a strong board of directors is critical—and we have a great one! As I have mentioned, accountability is key. Everyone should have someone they are accountable to.

I have mentored ministries that began as mom-and-pop operations with no staff. Most eventually reach a moment when they unconsciously decide they can't or won't grow. A small traveling ministry is fine—you can make an impact. But to influence the nations significantly, you need faith for provision and a determination to expand.

One example of pressing on in faith came when I called GOD TV to see if they would go live with a prayer meeting we were doing for California called PUSH—Pray Until Something Happens—which was held at the end of our Deborahs San Francisco event. Not only did that idea prove to be a great challenge—for reasons I'll explain—but the Deborahs San Francisco event itself was also quite difficult.

The hotel where PUSH took place was old and iconic, with a great ballroom and balconies, but it was located in the middle of one of the city's rough areas that was plagued by homelessness. When I went into the restroom upon arrival, I saw a person in a black lace dress. To my shock, he spoke with a man's voice. After I went into a stall, he banged on the door and shouted, "We know who you are—you and your b****es! You're not having a prayer meeting in our city. We're going to demonstrate!"

I had no idea what brought that on, as we had not said anything about the LGBTQ+ community in our promotions. We have never been haters of that community, but we do maintain a biblical stance on the issue. Three weeks before the event, a church that was originally going to host us had canceled on us, likely due to rumors spreading in the city. We prayed—hard. And when the day of the meeting came, no one showed up to demonstrate.

Another issue was our finances. We had no money, and our credit cards were maxed out from covering meeting expenses. Because of this, we couldn't even get our staff into the hotel or rent vans for our television equipment. We had handed out five-dollar bills to each staff member for the subway, and they were going to carry all our expensive equipment with them on foot. The day before we were to leave, my friend Pastor John Kilpatrick called and said, "Come preach for me this weekend!" The gift that resulted from that preaching engagement allowed us to pay down our credit cards so we could get our staff rooms in the hotel.

Then I got another call—this time from a pastor in the city who said, "Do you need to borrow the church van?" He even offered to pick up our crew. Saved by the Holy Spirit once again!

I always say, "Faith is always in the red!" I don't always like it, but it's just part of growing and expanding the Kingdom of God.

Doing Spiritual Battle in a War Zone

One of the most challenging assignments Mike and I have ever taken on was a trip to Iraq during the war. As I was praying for the war to end, I felt the Lord say, *I want you to go to Iraq and pray to turn the tide of the war—or it will become another Vietnam for America.*

Go to Iraq? I didn't know anyone there, or even know how to begin such an assignment! Yet the Lord also gave me a strategy:

Get as close to ancient Nineveh as possible. I did some studying and discovered that ancient Nineveh is now Mosul—which at the time was an extremely dangerous war zone. I had read reports of al-Qaeda beheading nuns there.

While researching, we met a young Egyptian man who had a pastor friend in Erbil, the city closest to Mosul. That was our open door. He knew how to get us there and had contacts. He also had a friend in Kuwait, where we could stop en route.

We asked others to join us, but in the end, only Dr. Sharon Stone and her husband, Greg Black, felt called to go on this divine adventure. (I left the word *dangerous* out of the invitations on purpose!)

Our team first flew into Jordan, where I preached in a packed church. I remember one remarkable moment when, during the meeting, I gave a word of knowledge and said, "Someone here thinks I'm a charlatan. Whoever that is, come up here now."

A man slowly made his way from the back of the church. I prophesied a clear and personal word over him that touched him so deeply that he gave his life to the Lord that night.

Then we were on our way to Kuwait. I will never forget the first time I looked out the plane window and saw the lights of Kuwait City—what many believe to be the cradle of civilization. We had no idea what to expect. We held meetings at the Christian compound there, which itself was spiritually significant from a pioneering missions perspective. The first night I preached, I suddenly asked, "Who were the first missionaries to Kuwait? I feel prayers coming from the ground of this place!"

No one knew the answer that night, but the next day they came back with the story. Many years ago, a young man named Samuel Zwemer felt called to establish a mission to Arabia. He applied to several missions organizations, but none wanted to risk sending someone to the Arabian Peninsula. So in June 1890, he went on his own.

It is believed that Zwemer made his way to Kuwait and would sit under a tree on a small hill, praying for the salvation of the nation. He kept getting kicked out, only to sneak back in. Eventually, he settled in Bahrain and started a mission there. He married his wife, Amy, a young missionary nurse, in 1896, and they served in the mission together. They had two small daughters who both died of dysentery. They buried them and marked the grave with a stone that read "Worthy is the Lord to receive treasures."

The Zwemers didn't leave Arabia after their daughters' deaths. They stayed. (They also were blessed with other children.) What Kuwaiti believers told me is that the very spot where the church compound we met in now stands is where Zwemer used to sit and pray for the salvation of Kuwait. That night, before we left for Iraq, I read his biography. I had been feeling trepidation, but after reading his story, much of my fear disappeared. Zwemer became known as the Apostle to Islam.

I wonder—what would the world be like if we had sent more missionaries to the Middle East? Today, only about 1 percent of the world's missionary force goes to Muslim nations.* If we can't go, we can at least pray!

In Kuwait, we rushed to the airport for the final leg of our journey. It was pitch black outside, and as I looked out the window of the plane, I realized we were descending sharply. I asked the flight attendant why we were dropping so fast into Erbil. She replied, "Oh, that's so they can't set their artillery sights on us. It's for our protection."

* This 1 percent statistic is often cited in missionary circles, although the percentage can change a little, depending on the specific report and year. It doesn't change much and is always a very low percentage.

Protection? I thought. *Oh no!* Mike was sleeping peacefully, but I was still battling fear. I was haunted by the thought that he hadn't particularly wanted to go to Iraq, but had said to me, "Honey, we've been married for thirty-six years. If we're going to die, we might as well die together." If he died, it would be my fault.

Then I looked over at our Egyptian friend. Another thought hit me: *He has small children! If he dies, they'll be fatherless!*

Suddenly, the Word of God I had planted in my soul over many years came to life. I declared out loud, "Devil, God has not given me a spirit of fear, but of power, love, and a sound mind!" And poof—the fear left. In its place was excitement.

We landed at the small Erbil airport and made our way to the customs line. Greg and Sharon started chatting with a tall, American-looking man who told them he was special ops. He instructed us to tell customs we didn't need visas—and that anyone with us didn't either.

As we approached the customs window, each of us handed over our passports. The officials didn't say a word. They simply pushed them back—unstamped—and waved us through. Suddenly, we were on the other side. But our Egyptian friend was pulled into another room. Now we had no Arabic translator and no one to help us navigate.

The entire process for us had taken just minutes. There was no barrier between customs and the baggage claim area. And the special ops soldier? Gone. To this day, we believe God sent an angel escort.

Eventually, our Egyptian friend was released, and we made our way outside—but no one was there to meet us. After some time, our contacts arrived and apologized profusely. They loaded us into black SUVs and drove us through the night.

When we arrived at the hotel, the reservation clerk shouted, "Movie stars are here! Movie stars are here!" We looked around, confused—until we realized he meant us. He had watched our TV show in Arabic.

The next day, Mike inquired about the price discrepancy between our hotel and the one across the street. The man pointed to the guards stationed around the building with AK-47s. That explained it.

We were scheduled to be in Iraq for only three days and hadn't planned on preaching, but the local church invited us to minister—and we did. The congregation included Kurds, Assyrians, Chaldeans, and Arabs. What a wonderful night of fellowship!

One woman approached me and said, "I'm the one you prophesied over during a Deborahs Company meeting, saying I should go to the Kurds in the north. I did it—we're building a training center now!"

The next day, to our surprise, a pastor drove up from Baghdad. He told us someone had given him my book *Possessing the Gates of the Enemy* in the early 2000s, and he had used it to establish a prayer network across Iraq. His story was incredible. He had been imprisoned by Saddam Hussein and was set to be executed. Then the United States bombed Baghdad, and in fear of the Americans, his captors let him go.

After that meeting, we drove as close to ancient Nineveh as we could. It was too dangerous to go into the city itself. We found a windswept hill nearby, prayed, and asked God to turn the tide of the war. We also prayed at a park near a ziggurat built by the ancient Assyrian King Sennacherib, whom the Bible mentions. Armed guards were posted throughout the park, so Mike distracted them while we prayed. We even prayed where statues of false gods had been erected—waiting until midnight to avoid crowds.

We flew out early the next morning. One of our team members had picked up rocks, which delayed us at the airport. We're not sure why the airport's security people objected to the rocks, but eventually they let us take them on the plane. At last we boarded, and when the wheels lifted off, we all breathed a sigh of relief.

What was the fruit of our trip? Of course, ministry to the Body of Christ. And our connection with the pastor from Baghdad. Were our prayers answered? Yes. There was a military surge and a change in generals that turned the tide—for a time. It also stopped the tide of terrorism for a season.

Could we make this kind of journey for every war? No. We went to Iraq due to a *specific* word from the Lord for a *specific* moment. Along those lines, I will add a disclaimer here: We do *not* encourage others to do the kinds of things we did without a *clear directive* from the Lord. As watchmen, we must listen to Him and obey. Sometimes it requires a corporate forty-day fast—or longer. Every situation is different. It might take much more intercessory prayer, depending on the situation. There are certain assignments the Lord will give us for nations, and those of us on the team who went to Iraq were not novices. We were following His lead, as all those called to nations must do in order to be effective for the Kingdom.

Lucy's Well in Kenya

One of the nations God has assigned Mike and me to is Kenya. We have had close governmental ties there. We have given significant prophecies for that nation through the years. On one trip, we went to the Maasai Mara National Reserve, a game preserve in southwest Kenya. I thought we were going on a little vacation. However, after going to a local village and seeing that the people had no water, I was so disturbed I couldn't sleep. Then, when I found out the women were walking five miles or so to draw water and some were being killed by lions and elephants as they went, I really couldn't sleep!

I asked the country's First Lady where we could find someone reputable to drill a well, and she made a recommendation. We also had met an influential young leader named Moses, and he worked to get land given to us for a well. This water project was very important to me because my sister, Lucy, had always dreamed of drilling a well in Africa, as her husband's family owned a drilling company.

In the end, we drilled Lucy's Well, and five thousand people migrated to be near this source of clean water. We also built a prayer garden and other projects to help the locals near the well, like restrooms and showers. It has been very fulfilling!

Holy Spirit adventures like the ones I have told you about are challenging, exciting, and at times dangerous. Don't go without confirmation. If it is your first time, seek multiple counselors and build a strong prayer team to back you.

22

Leaving a Legacy

One thing important to both Mike and me is legacy. Beyond telling our story, we want to leave behind everything we have learned by both being mentored and mentoring others—hence this book. We have learned from some of the greatest leaders on earth and have survived ministry as a couple—that's saying a lot!

When Mike and I had our fiftieth anniversary, we did something really special. We had a full-blown renewal ceremony with our whole family of children and grandchildren. Remember that the first time, we had a home wedding at Miss Maben's house. Back then, Mike and I didn't get to have what I had always dreamed of for a wedding. So this time around we did the whole thing!

When we looked for a facility for our ceremony, I wanted something historic, with a pipe organ. That was important to me, and we got it all—in a one-hundred-year-old church in Oak Cliff, Texas, the same city where my parents had gotten married!

The church has gorgeous stained-glass windows, with a beautiful stained-glass rotunda at the top.

I wore a beautiful bridal gown with a long train. Mike was gorgeous in his tuxedo. All of our family looked incredible. Our grandsons were ushers and ring bearers, and my only granddaughter was the flower girl.

We also had some of our best friends take part in the ceremony. Our dear friend James Goll had a dream that he sang "The Lord's Prayer" in the ceremony, and he did—beautifully! Chuck Pierce performed the ceremony, along with our pastor, Jim Hennesy. Ed Silvoso, our longtime buddy whom we worked with on transformation projects in Argentina, walked me down the aisle, to the swelling of the magnificent pipe organ playing. I sort of feel as though Daddy was smiling down from heaven on that. Our prophet friends prophesied, and I felt it was heavenly—simply divine! Thank you to the Generals International staff, and especially to Jenay Carlucci Jacobs, for all their hard work and amazing execution.

Mike and I looked at each other during the renewal ceremony with new eyes, and it was very romantic. I recommend it for all couples. It was a renewal of our vows for the next twenty-plus years!

A Few Final Thoughts

This leads into a new topic I want to share about briefly before we end. No one talks about aging while in ministry, but it should be talked about more. Mike and I both agree on one thing: Retirement isn't in the Bible. We don't plan to retire. We will go one-hundred-percent until we step into heaven. We'd like to go together—but that is up to the Lord.

As I have mentioned, we must all work at staying emotionally whole as we serve the Lord. In particular, there is an emotional toll that comes with prophesying. People will call you a false prophet or a Jezebel. Cessationists will post cruel comments. My advice? Don't read such comments regularly! And when they do reach you, forgive and pray for the people who are the source of them.

We must also all stay accountable. It is important to have leaders in place whom you check in with during controversies. Some controversial situations will require a response, and the input from those you are accountable to will be valuable. In other situations, they may just encourage you and confirm you need to let God fight your battles. He's really good at it!

To those who have longed for a mentor—this book is for you. To those who are simply hungry for more of God—this book is for you. It has been a labor of love to write it, my attempt to leave behind the legacy we have carried.

A Prayer for You

Let me pray for you as we finish our time talking about the life lessons I have learned:

> *Lord, I pray for Your child as they seek to follow Your will and purpose for their life. Give them courage to grow in every season, and fulfill every purpose You created them for. Let them hold nothing back, and may they one day hear You say, "Well done, good and faithful servant." In Jesus' name, Amen.*

I pray that you have enjoyed journeying with me through my life. Of course, I keep thinking, *Oh, I forgot this and that. . . .* But most of the highlights are here. I want to keep on having supernatural adventures and learning more about God every day of my life, until I step over into glory. The same is true for Mike, and may it also be true for you. May the Lord use you mightily as you fulfill your purpose on His earth.

Acknowledgments

Thank You, Lord, for all You have done for me. It is the honor of my life to serve You and be a minister of the gospel.

To my family, I'm not complete without you! Thank you to my son and daughter-in-law, Daniel and Jenay, for lovingly nudging me to write it all down! My beautiful daughter, Mary (aka Kyrin), you are so special! To my grandchildren, Lilli, Liam, Wyatt, Malachi, Caden, and their spouses, and Zion, and to my great-grandchildren, Qesqah and Eden, and one more on the way! You are my legacy!

My brother, Richard, who was a professor for twenty-five years in China, is an encouragement to me. I am grateful I had my little sister, Lucy, for fifty-six years before she went to heaven. I am also grateful to her husband, Mark, who remains a friend to this day.

My deepest gratitude to the intercessory teams for Generals International, our former prayer leaders, Robert and Juana Griffin, and to Abe Ali and his team for praying through this writing. Also, my longtime friend Timmerle Kelly, and the staff of Generals International. You all have been cheerleaders for me! Thanks to my assistant, Asher Mian, for your work editing.

I also want to specifically acknowledge some of my dearest friends, Russ and Julie Zylstra, Hal and Cheryl Sacks, Chuck and Pam Pierce, Steve and Stephanie Fullerton, Ché and Sue Ahn, and Dutch and Ceci Sheets. Old friends are good friends! In addition, my pastors, Jim and Becky Hennesy. Doris Wagner, you are always in my heart! All of us have lived a lot of life together!

I also want to thank Chosen Books, whose editors believed in me when I wrote *Possessing the Gates of the Enemy* when nobody knew me, and took a chance on publishing my book. Thank you for helping send the message of intercessory prayer around the world. Kim Bangs, you helped me get this book of memoirs done and helped me leave a legacy. Thank you!

CINDY JACOBS is a prophet, speaker, teacher, and author with a heart for discipling nations in the areas of prayer and the prophetic. She and her husband, Mike, are the founders of Generals International, working to achieve social transformation through intercession and prophetic ministry. Cindy has written several bestselling books, including *Possessing the Gates of the Enemy*, *The Essential Guide to Prayer*, and *The Power of Persistent Prayer*. Cindy and Mike have a show called *Double Portion* that is streamed around the world through Instagram and Facebook. She travels and speaks internationally to groups of hundreds of thousands each year in churches and conference centers. Cindy and Mike have two grown children and six grandchildren and reside near Dallas, Texas.

CONNECT WITH CINDY

Generals.org

@CindyJacobsOfficial

@CindyMJacobs

@CindyJacobs